Gravy

Delicious Gravy's Prepared Simply for
All Types of Meals

By
BookSumo Press
All rights reserved

Published by
http://www.booksumo.com

ENJOY THE RECIPES?

KEEP ON COOKING
WITH 6 MORE FREE COOKBOOKS!

Visit our website and simply enter your email address to join the club and receive your 6 cookbooks.

http://booksumo.com/magnet

https://www.instagram.com/booksumopress/

https://www.facebook.com/booksumo/

LEGAL NOTES

All Rights Reserved. No Part Of This Book May Be Reproduced Or Transmitted In Any Form Or By Any Means. Photocopying, Posting Online, And / Or Digital Copying Is Strictly Prohibited Unless Written Permission Is Granted By The Book's Publishing Company. Limited Use Of The Book's Text Is Permitted For Use In Reviews Written For The Public.

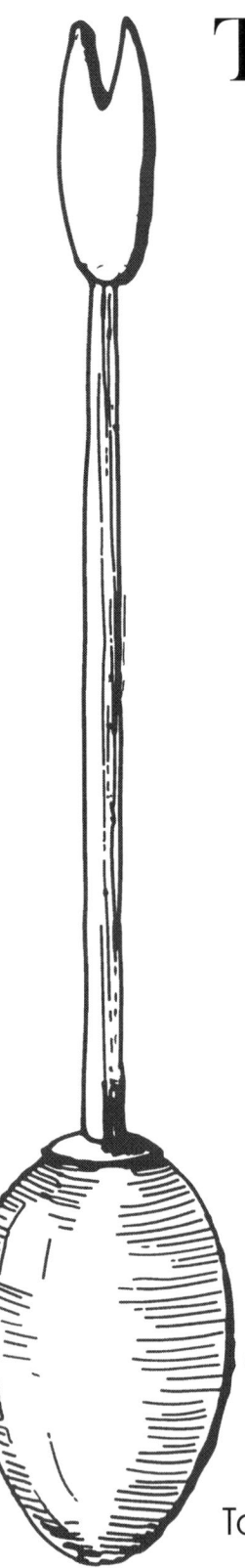

Table of Contents

How to Make a Gravy 9

Potato Gravy 10

American Gravy 11

Sweet Roasted Gravy 12

25-Minute Chicken in Gravy 13

2-Beef Gravy 14

Real Southern Gizzard Gravy 15

Gravy for Vegetarians 16

Alternative Gravy (Au Jus) 17

Herbed Worchester Gravy 18

Hot Mashed Potatoes w Gravy 19

Pastoral Fields Gravy 20

Gravy in Charlotte 21

Pennsylvania Beef Gravy 22

White Gravy 23

Chicken Curry with Karachi Gravy 24

Baked Gravy 26

Tomato Gravy Ground Beef on Toast 27

Meatballs w/ Gravy 28

Simple Southern Gravy 29

Cream of Gravy 30

Megan's Make-Ahead Gravy 31

European Meatballs in Gravy 32

Gravy Potatoes with Sausage 33

Simple Cornstarch Gravy 34

Beef Broth Based Gravy 35

Dairy-Free Gravy 36

Mexican Masa Harina Gravy 37

Gravy Rustica 38

Rojo Gravy over Burritos 39

Herbed Gravy 41

Carolina Gravy w Buttermilk Biscuits 42

10-Minute Gravy 43

Sweet Roasted Turkey with Gravy 44

Amish Friendship Gravy 46

2-Ingredient Tangy Gravy 47

Spokane Nutty Gravy 48

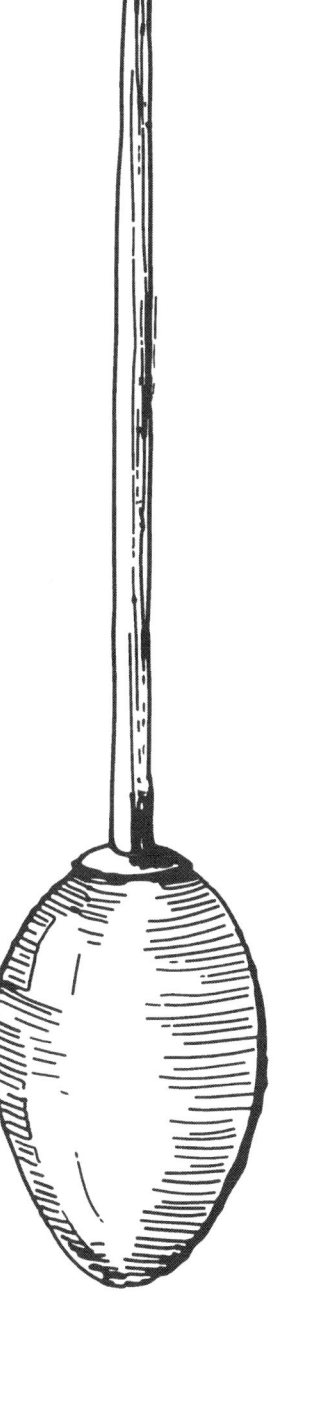

Gravy Skillet 49

Arkansas Fried Chicken 50

Guyanese Jumbo Shrimp with Gravy 51

Tallahassee Country Gravy 52

Marjoram Wheat Gravy 53

Gravy Spice Mix 54

Beef Croquettes w Curry Gravy 55

Easy Egg Gravy 57

How to Make Glazed Lamb Chops 58

Alabama Gravy for Biscuits 59

Chicago Top Roast with Spicy Gravy 60

Turkey Burgers with Gravy 62

Kentucky Liver and Onions 63

American Cornstarch Gravy 64

Spicy Tomato Gravy from Ghana 65

5-Ingredient Garlicky Gravy 66

Mexi-Cajun Steak with Gravy 67

Salisbury Steaks 69

Onion Mushroom Gravy 70

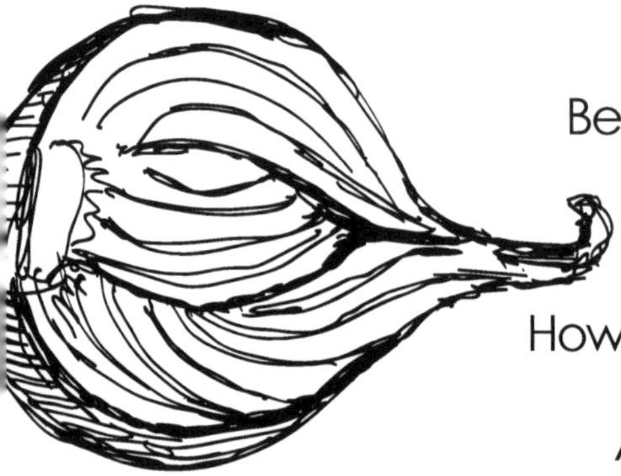

Onion Mushroom Gravy 71

Food Court Gravy 72

3-Ingredient Gravy 73

Raw Vegan Gravy 74

Shreveport Gravy 75

Creamy Gouda Lunch Box 76

Caribbean Gravy 77

Rocky Mount Bean Gravy 78

Croquettes with Cremini Gravy 79

Plain Yogurt Gravy 81

Vegan Comfort Food (Biscuits with Gravy) 82

Gravy in College 84

Dairy-Free Gravy 85

German Gingersnap Gravy 86

Pan Fried Gravy 87

Mexican Chocolate Gravy 88

Curried Seafood Gravy 89

April Egg Gravy 90

Garlicky Spuds with Gravy 91

5-Ingredient Gravy 92

Birmingham Gravy 93

45-Minute Chicken w Gravy 94

Baked Chicken Cutlets w Gravy 95

Amelia's Turkey with Country Gravy 96

Japanese Mushroom Gravy 99

Nutty Garlic Gravy 100

Mushroom Gravy 101

Corned Beef with Irish Gravy 102

Red Gravy 104

Apple Roasted Turkey w Vinegar Gravy 105

How to Make a Gravy

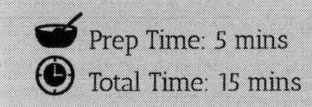

🥣 Prep Time: 5 mins
🕐 Total Time: 15 mins

Servings per Recipe: 1
Calories   555.6 kcal
Fat   47.4 g
Cholesterol   122.0 mg
Sodium   2772.9 mg
Carbohydrates   24.4 g
Protein   9.2 g

Ingredients

1/4 C. butter
1/4 C. flour
2 C. beef broth
1/4 tsp salt
1/4 tsp pepper
1 tsp Kitchen Bouquet (browning sauce)

Directions

1. In a pot, add the butter over medium heat and cook until melted.
2. Add the flour, beating continuously until smooth.
3. Stir in the salt and pepper and cook for 4-5 minutes, mixing continuously.
4. Set the heat to low.
5. Gradually, pour the broth, mixing continuously until smooth.
6. Add the kitchen bouquet and set the heat to medium.
7. Cook until desired thickness, mixing continuously.
8. Enjoy hot.

POTATO
Gravy

Prep Time: 5 mins
Total Time: 15 mins

Servings per Recipe: 8
Calories	18.3 kcal
Fat	0.1 g
Cholesterol	0.0 mg
Sodium	388.3 mg
Carbohydrates	3.5 g
Protein	1.1 g

Ingredients

3 C. fat free chicken broth
1 (10 oz.) cans mushroom stems and pieces
1/4 tsp black pepper
1 tsp granulated garlic powder
1 tsp chicken soup base

1 tsp soy sauce
1 tsp Worcestershire sauce
4 tbsp instant potato flakesw

Directions

1. In a pot, add the mushrooms with liquid and broth and cook until boiling.
2. Add the Worcestershire sauce, soy sauce, pepper, chicken soup base, garlic powder and black pepper and mix well.
3. Stir in the potato flakes and cook until desired thickness, mixing continuously.
4. Enjoy hot..

American Gravy

Prep Time: 5 mins
Total Time: 15 mins

Servings per Recipe: 2
Calories	94.9 kcal
Fat	8.4 g
Cholesterol	10.1 mg
Sodium	38.9 mg
Carbohydrates	4.7 g
Protein	0.36 g

Ingredients

- 2 C. water
- 1 tsp beef bouillon
- 1/4 tsp ground black pepper
- 1/4 tsp Kitchen Bouquet (browning sauce)
- 2 tbsp butter
- 1/2 tsp garlic powder
- 1/8 tsp onion powder
- 2 tbsp cornstarch
- 2 tbsp cold water

Directions

1. For the gravy: in a pan, add all the ingredients and cook until boiling.
2. Meanwhile, in bowl, dissolve the cornstarch in cold water.
3. Gradually, add the cornstarch mixture, mixing conspicuously and then, cook for about 2-3 minutes.
4. Enjoy hot.

SWEET
Roasted Gravy

Prep Time: 30 mins
Total Time: 40 mins

Servings per Recipe: 1
Calories   227.8 kcal
Fat   10.1 g
Cholesterol   0.0 mg
Sodium   121.3 mg
Carbohydrates   32.7 g
Protein   3.7 g

Ingredients

8 -10 oz. onions, peeled and chopped
1/2 tsp ground paprika
2 tsp peanut oil, divided
1 tsp caster sugar
2 tsp Worcestershire sauce
1 tsp mustard powder

15 fluid oz. vegetable stock
2 tsp plain flour
salt & ground black pepper

Directions

1. Set your oven to 400 degrees F before doing anything else.
2. In a bowl, add the onions, 1 tsp of the oil, sugar and paprika and toss to coat well.
3. In the bottom of a 13x9-inch baking dish, arrange the onion pieces.
4. Cook in the oven for about 15-20 minutes.
5. Remove from the oven and keep aside.
6. In a bowl, add the stock, Worcestershire and mustard powder and mix well.
7. In a pot, add the remaining oil and cooked onion over medium heat and mix well.
8. Add the plain flour and stir to combine.
9. Cook for about 2 minutes, mixing well.
10. Slowly, add the stock, beating continuously.
11. Cook until boiling.
12. Cook for about 4-5 minutes.
13. Stir in the salt and pepper and enjoy hot..

25-Minute Chicken in Creamy Gravy Dinner

Prep Time: 5 mins
Total Time: 25 mins

Servings per Recipe: 4
Calories	486.1 kcal
Fat	31.0 g
Cholesterol	143.0 mg
Sodium	811.2 mg
Carbohydrates	21.2 g
Protein	30.3 g

Ingredients

- 1/2 C. flour
- 2 tsp paprika
- 1 tsp salt
- 1 tsp pepper
- 1 tsp garlic powder
- 1 tsp cayenne pepper
- 4 boneless skinless chicken breasts
- 1/4 C. butter
- 1 (10 1/2 oz.) cans cream of chicken soup
- 1/4 C. sliced green onion
- 8 oz. sour cream

Directions

1. In a re-sealable bag, add the chicken, flour and seasonings.
2. Seal the bag and shake to coat well.
3. In a wok, add the butter and cook until melted.
4. Add the chicken and cook for about 4-5 minutes on both sides.
5. Add the onion and soup and stir to combine.
6. Set the heat to low and simmer, covered for about 9-10 minutes.
7. Stir in the sour cream a remove from the heat.
8. Enjoy hot.

2-BEEF Gravy

Prep Time: 15 mins
Total Time: 40 mins

Servings per Recipe: 8
Calories   159.4 kcal
Fat   10.7 g
Cholesterol   38.5 mg
Sodium   305.0 mg
Carbohydrates   3.7 g
Protein   11.3 g

Ingredients

1 lb. ground beef
1 can cream of mushroom soup
1/2 small onion, minced
salt & pepper
1 tbsp flour
1 tsp beef bouillon

Directions

1. Heat a wok ad cook the ground beef until browned completely.
2. Drain the grease completely.
3. Add the onion, soup, beef bouillon, salt, pepper and 1 1/2-1 3/4 can of water and stir to combine.
4. Set the heat to low and cook for about 18-20 minutes.
5. Stir in the flour and cook for about, stirring continuously.
6. Enjoy hot..

Real Southern Gizzard Gravy

🥣 Prep Time: 10 mins
🕐 Total Time: 3 hrs 15 mins

Servings per Recipe: 1
Calories	37.7 kcal
Fat	0.5 g
Cholesterol	9.6 mg
Sodium	13.8 mg
Carbohydrates	6.7 g
Protein	1.6 g

Ingredients

- 1 turkey giblets, neck, gizzard and liver
- salt and pepper
- 1 tsp sage
- 1 stalk celery, chopped
- 1 small onion, chopped
- 2 - 4 tbsp seasoned flour
- water

Directions

1. In a pot, add the turkey giblets, onion, celery, sage, salt, pepper and enough water to cover and cook until boiling.
2. Set the heat to low and cook, covered for about 2 1/2 - 3 hours.
3. Through a strainer, strain the liquid into a bowl.
4. Chop the gizzard and liver.
5. Remove the meat from the turkey neck bones.
6. In a food processor, add the strained cooking liquid, neck meat, chopped gizzard and liver and pulse until smooth.
7. Add the flour, salt and pepper and pulse until well combined.
8. Remove the turkey from the roaster.
9. Now, set your oven to 450 degrees F.
10. Remove the fat from the roasting pan, leaving the brown bits and juice into the pan.
11. With a wire whisk, beat the contents present in roasting pan.
12. In the roasting pan, add the pureed mixture and beat until well combined.
13. Add some water, stirring continuously.
14. Place the roasting pan in the oven and cook for about 15 minutes.
15. Remove from the oven and enjoy hot.

GRAVY
for Vegetarians

Prep Time: 5 mins
Total Time: 20 mins

Servings per Recipe: 1
Calories   213.9 kcal
Fat   17.1 g
Cholesterol   0.0 mg
Sodium   1209.6 mg
Carbohydrates   12.0 g
Protein   3.5 g

Ingredients

3 tbsp margarine
2 tbsp chopped onions
2 minced garlic cloves
3 tbsp flour
2 tbsp soy sauce
1 C. water

salt and pepper

Directions

1. In a pan, add the margarine over medium-high heat and cook until melted.
2. Add the onion and garlic and stir fry for about 4-5 minutes.
3. Now, set the heat to medium.
4. For the roux: slowly, add the flour, mixing constantly.
5. Add the water and soy sauce, mixing continuously.
6. Stir in the salt and pepper and cook until desired thickness of gravy.
7. Enjoy hot..

Alternative Gravy (Au Jus)

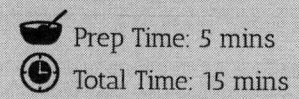

- Prep Time: 5 mins
- Total Time: 15 mins

Servings per Recipe: 4
Calories	1.7 kcal
Fat	0.0 g
Cholesterol	0.0 mg
Sodium	101.7 mg
Carbohydrates	0.2 g
Protein	0.2 g

Ingredients

3 C. water
4 tsp beef bouillon
1 tsp soy sauce
1/4 tsp garlic powder
salt and pepper

Directions

1. In a pot, add and cook until boiling.
2. Set the heat to low and add the beef bouillon, stirring continuously.
3. Add the garlic powder, soy sauce, salt and pepper and stir to combine.
4. Cook until desired thickness.
5. Enjoy hot.

HERBED
Worchester Gravy

Prep Time: 5 mins
Total Time: 30 mins

Servings per Recipe: 4
Calories	115.4 kcal
Fat	7.9 g
Cholesterol	2.7 mg
Sodium	144.1 mg
Carbohydrates	8.3 g
Protein	2.8 g

Ingredients

2 tbsp vegetable oil
1 large onion, halved
1 tbsp plain flour
12 fluid oz. chicken stock
1 tsp dried mixed herbs
1 tsp Worcestershire sauce

Directions

1. In a pot, add the oil and cook until heated.
2. Add the onions and cook for about 9-10 minutes, stirring frequently.
3. Add the flour and cook for about 3 minutes, mixing continuously.
4. Stir in the herbs, Worcestershire sauce and stock and cook until mixture becomes slightly thick.
5. Cover the pot slightly and cook for about 12-15 minutes, mixing occasionally.
6. Enjoy hot..

Hot Mashed Potatoes with Gravy

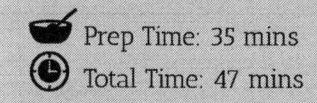

🥣 Prep Time: 35 mins
🕐 Total Time: 47 mins

Servings per Recipe: 1
Calories   373.4 kcal
Fat   23.1 g
Cholesterol   102.8 mg
Sodium   616.9 mg
Carbohydrates   8.9 g
Protein   30.6 g

Ingredients

- 1 lb. ground beef
- 1 (14 1/2 oz.) cans beef broth, divided
- 1 small onion, chopped
- 2 tbsp dried parsley flakes
- 1 tbsp dried basil
- 1 tsp garlic powder
- 1 tsp seasoning salt
- 1/2 tsp pepper
- 2 tbsp cornstarch
- hot mashed potatoes

Directions

1. Heat a wok and cook the beef until no more pink.
2. Drain the grease from the wok.
3. Add 1 1/2 C. of the broth and stir to combine.
4. Add the onion, herbs, seasoned salt, garlic powder and pepper and cook for about 7-10 minutes.
5. In a small bowl, dissolve the cornstarch in remaining broth.
6. Stir the cornstarch mixture into the beef mixture and cook until boiling.
7. Cook for about 3 minutes, mixing continuously.
8. Enjoy hot over mashed potatoes.

PASTORAL
Fields Gravy

Prep Time: 5 mins
Total Time: 25 mins

Servings per Recipe: 1
Calories	786.0 kcal
Fat	58.7 g
Cholesterol	179.8 mg
Sodium	1456.0 mg
Carbohydrates	18.6 g
Protein	42.9 g

Ingredients

1 lb. bulk breakfast sausage
1/4 C. flour
2 C. milk
salt and pepper

Directions

1. Heat a heavy-bottomed wok and cook the sausage until browned completely.
2. With a slotted spoon, transfer the cooked sausage into a bowl.
3. Remove the grease from the wok, leaving 2 tbsp inside.
4. In the same wok, add the flour over low heat, beating continuously.
5. Cook for about 5 minutes, mixing continuously.
6. Remove from the heat.
7. Slowly, add the milk, beating continuously until smooth.
8. Place the pan over medium-high heat and cook until boiling, mixing often.
9. Stir in the cooked sausage, salt and black pepper and remove from the heat.
10. Enjoy hot..

Gravy in Charlotte

Prep Time: 7 mins
Total Time: 7 mins

Servings per Recipe: 4
Calories   145.0 kcal
Fat   10.3 g
Cholesterol   32.3 mg
Sodium   401.4 mg
Carbohydrates   9.0 g
Protein   4.5 g

Ingredients

2 tbsp butter
2 tbsp flour
2 C. milk
1 tsp poultry seasoning
1/2 tsp salt
1/2 tsp pepper, ground

Directions

1. In a pot, add the butter over medium heat and cook until melted.
2. Add the flour and beat until smooth.
3. Cook for about 1 minute, stirring continuously.
4. Add the milk, beating continuously until smooth.
5. Cook until boiling, beating continuously.
6. Enjoy hot.

PENNSYLVANIA
Beef Gravy

Prep Time: 5 mins
Total Time: 20 mins

Servings per Recipe: 4
Calories   232.7 kcal
Fat   13.0 g
Cholesterol   63.2 mg
Sodium   931.4 mg
Carbohydrates   13.7 g
Protein   15.4 g

Ingredients

1/4 lb. dried beef, chopped (jerky)
2 tbsp butter
3 tbsp flour
3 C. milk

Directions

1. In a wok, add the butter and cook until melted.
2. Stir in the dried beef pieces and stir fry until golden brown.
3. Add the flour and stir until smooth.
4. Slowly, add the milk, mixing continuously until smooth.
5. Set the heat to low and cook until desired thickness.
6. Enjoy hot..

White Gravy

Prep Time: 5 mins
Total Time: 20 mins

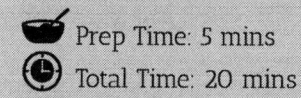

Servings per Recipe: 4
Calories	482.3 kcal
Fat	36.4 g
Cholesterol	34.1 mg
Sodium	120.0 mg
Carbohydrates	29.2 g
Protein	10.4 g

Ingredients

1/2 C. vegetable oil
3/4 C. flour
1 tsp seasoning salt
black pepper
4 C. milk

Directions

1. In a wok, add the oil over medium heat and cook until heated.
2. Add the flour, salt and pepper beating continuously until well combined.
3. Cook for about 10 minutes, mixing frequently.
4. Slowly, add the milk, beating continuously.
5. Cook until desired thickness, string frequently.
6. Enjoy hot.

CHICKEN
Curry with Karachi Gravy

Prep Time: 20 mins
Total Time: 1 hr 15 mins

Servings per Recipe: 2
Calories	1293.8 kcal
Fat	109.4 g
Cholesterol	170.1 mg
Sodium	362.1 mg
Carbohydrates	34.7 g
Protein	49.6 g

Ingredients

1 lb. chicken, cubed
1 onion, chopped
2 tsp curry powder
2 tsp chili powder
2 chopped cayenne chili
4 cloves crushed garlic
2 inches ginger root, grated
5 tbsp vegetable oil
4 tbsp roughly chopped coriander leaves
1 tbsp whole coriander leaves
1 tsp garam masala
1/2 coconut, grated
1/2 C. coconut milk
Gravy
1 onion, sliced
4 cloves garlic, chopped
6 tomatoes, blanched peeled, cored and quartered
1 tsp turmeric powder
2 tsp chili powder
1 tsp garam masala powder
4 green cardamom pods
4 tbsp vegetable oil
1 C. water
1 pinch salt

Directions

1. For paste: in a bowl, add the curry powder, chili powder and a little water and mix well.
2. For the masala gravy: in a skillet, heat the oil over medium heat.
3. Add the tomatoes, onion and garlic and cook for about 8-9 minutes, stirring occasionally.
4. Add half of the water and cook for about 6 minutes.
5. Stir in the spices and remaining water and cook for about 4 minutes, mixing continuously
6. Remove from the heat and keep aside to cool.
7. In a blender, add the mixture and pulse until smooth.
8. In a skillet, heat the oil over medium heat and sauté the onion for about 4-5 minutes.
9. Add the ginger, garlic and chili and sauté for about 5 minutes.
10. Add the paste and sauté for about 30 seconds.

11. Add the chicken pieces and stir to combine well.
12. Add half of the coconut, masala gravy, and coconut milk and cook for about 18-20 minutes, mixing frequently.
13. Enjoy hot..

BAKED Gravy

Prep Time: 5 mins
Total Time: 2 hrs 5 mins

Servings per Recipe: 6
Calories	1091.2 kcal
Fat	110.5 g
Cholesterol	150.2 mg
Sodium	1100.7 mg
Carbohydrates	9.1 g
Protein	13.9 g

Ingredients

2 lb. boneless beef cubes
1 (10 1/2 oz.) cans cream of mushroom soup
1 (10 1/2 oz.) cans water
1 (1 7/8 oz.) envelopes dry onion soup mix

Directions

1. Set your oven to 325 degrees F before doing anything else.
2. In a bowl, add the water and soups and with an electric mixer, mix until well combined.
3. In a baking dish, add the beef cubes and soup mixture and mix well.
4. Cover the baking dish and cook in the oven for about 2 hours, mixing 5-6 times.
5. Enjoy hot..

Tomato Gravy Ground Beef on Toast

Prep Time: 30 mins
Total Time: 30 mins

Servings per Recipe: 10
Calories   182.6 kcal
Fat   10.4 g
Cholesterol   46.2 mg
Sodium   92.1 mg
Carbohydrates   8.0 g
Protein   13.8 g

Ingredients

- 1 1/2 lb. ground beef
- 2 medium onions, chopped
- cooking oil
- salt and pepper
- 5 tbsp flour
- 1 (16 oz.) cans whole tomatoes, diced
- 5 1/2 oz. tomato juice
- 2 C. hot water
- 1/2 tsp ground nutmeg
- 1/2 tsp sugar

Directions

1. Heat a wok and cook the crumbled beef and onion until beef has no more pink.
2. Set the heat to low.
3. Slowly, add the flour, beating continuously until smooth.
4. Add the tomato juice, tomatoes and water and cook until desired thickness of the gravy.
5. Stir in the sugar and nutmeg and enjoy hot.

THURSDAY'S
European Dinner (Meatballs with Gravy)

Prep Time: 15 mins
Total Time: 30 mins

Servings per Recipe: 4
Calories	455.7 kcal
Fat	34.4 g
Cholesterol	147.4 mg
Sodium	1009.3 mg
Carbohydrates	10.9 g
Protein	24.3 g

Ingredients

1 1/2 lb. ground beef round
1 C. soft breadcrumbs
1/3 C. water
1/4 C. minced green onion
1 egg
2 tsp salt, divided

1/4 tsp pepper
1/4 C. butter
3 tbsp flour
2 C. milk
2 tbsp chopped dill

Directions

1. Set your oven to 400 degrees F before doing anything else.
2. In a bowl, add the beef, egg, breadcrumbs, onions, water, 1 1/2 tsp of the salt and pepper and mix until well combined.
3. Make 24 equal sized meatballs from the mixture.
4. In the bottom of a jelly-roll pan, arrange the meatballs in a single layer.
5. Cook in the oven for about 15 minutes.
6. Meanwhile, in a pan, add the butter and cook until melted.
7. Stir in the flour and cook until just boiling.
8. Remove from the heat and slowly, add the milk, mixing continuously until smooth.
9. Place the pan over heat and cook until desired thickness, mixing continuously.
10. Stir in the dill and remaining salt and remove from the heat.
11. Divide the meatballs onto serving plates.
12. Top with the gravy and enjoy..

Simple Southern Gravy

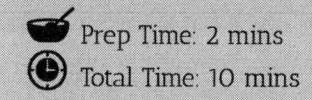

🥣 Prep Time: 2 mins
🕐 Total Time: 10 mins

Servings per Recipe: 8
Calories   71.4 kcal
Fat   5.4 g
Cholesterol   13.3 mg
Sodium   449.7 mg
Carbohydrates   3.8 g
Protein   1.7 g

Ingredients

50 g butter
5 tbsp all-purpose flour
drippings from turkey
2 C. chicken broth
3/4 tsp salt
 ground pepper
1 dash, browning

Directions

1. In a pot, add the butter and cook until melted.
2. Add the flour, mixing continuously until smooth.
3. Slowly, add the chicken broth, mixing well until smooth.
4. Cook until desired thickness of the gravy.
5. Stir in the salt and pepper and browning enjoy hot.

CREAM of Gravy

Prep Time: 2 mins
Total Time: 10 mins

Servings per Recipe: 4
Calories   167.4 kcal
Fat   13.2 g
Cholesterol   0.0 mg
Sodium   919.4 mg
Carbohydrates   9.7 g
Protein   2.8 g

Ingredients

3 tbsp margarine
3 tbsp flour
1 (10 3/4 oz.) cans beef broth
3/4 C. water
1 (10 3/4 oz.) cans cream of mushroom soup

Directions

1. In a pot, add the margarine and cook until melted.
2. Add the flour, mixing continuously until well combined.
3. Gradually, add the broth and water, mixing continuously.
4. Cook until boiling.
5. Add the soup and cook until heated completely, mixing continuously.
6. Enjoy hot..

Megan's Make-Ahead Gravy

Prep Time: 15 mins
Total Time: 40 mins

Servings per Recipe: 4
Calories   51.8 kcal
Fat   3.1 g
Cholesterol   7.6 mg
Sodium   4.9 mg
Carbohydrates   5.3 g
Protein   1.3 g

Ingredients

1/2 oz. unsalted butter
1 small onion, chopped
1/4 lb. mushroom, sliced
1 low-sodium bouillon cube
10 fluid oz. hot water
2 tbsp corn flour, blended with a little cold water

salt and black pepper

Directions

1. In a pot, add the butter and cook until melted.
2. Add the mushrooms and onion and cook for about 7-8 minutes, stirring frequently.
3. In a bowl, add the stock cube and hot water and mix well.
4. Stir the cube mixture into gravy, stirring continuously.
5. Add the corn flour mixture, beating continuously until smooth.
6. Enjoy hot.

EUROPEAN
Meatballs in Gravy

Prep Time: 10 mins
Total Time: 25 mins

Servings per Recipe: 4
Calories   332.9 kcal
Fat   27.4 g
Cholesterol   62.1 mg
Sodium   812.9 mg
Carbohydrates   18.8 g
Protein   5.5 g

Ingredients

1/2 large onion, chopped
1 tbsp minced garlic
1 (1 oz.) envelope onion soup mix
1 (16 oz.) containers sour cream
1 tbsp Hungarian paprika
2 tbsp dried parsley
2 tbsp beef base
2 tbsp Worcestershire sauce
1 (7 oz.) cans mushrooms, drained
3 C. water
2 tbsp cornstarch
2 lb. frozen precooked meatballs
1 tbsp olive oil

Directions

1. In a heavy-bottomed pan, add the oil and cook until heated.
2. Add the onion and cook for about -5 minutes.
3. Add the garlic and cook for cook for 30 seconds.
4. Add the soup mix, 3 C. of the water, paprika, soup base and Worcestershire sauce and stir to combine.
5. Add the meatballs and gently, stir to combine.
6. Set the heat to medium-high and cook for about 13-15 minutes.
7. Add the mushrooms, parsley and sour cream and stir to combine.
8. In a bowl, dissolve the cornstarch into 1/4 C. of the water.
9. Slowly, add the cornstarch mixture into gravy, mixing continuously.
10. Cook until desired thickness of the gravy
11. Enjoy hot..

Monday's Dinner (Gravy Potatoes with Sausage)

🍲 Prep Time: 45 mins
🕐 Total Time: 45 mins

Servings per Recipe: 6
Calories	551.4 kcal
Fat	28.3 g
Cholesterol	110.4 mg
Sodium	784.5 mg
Carbohydrates	45.9 g
Protein	27.8 g

Ingredients

2 lb. raw link sausage
7 medium potatoes, peeled and chopped
1 large onion, cut into rings
2 C. water
salt
pepper

Directions

1. Heat a lightly greased pan over medium-high heat and cook the sausage until browned.
2. Add the sliced onion and cook for some time.
3. Add the potatoes, water, salt and pepper and stir to combine.
4. Set the heat to medium low and simmer until desired doneness of the potatoes.
5. Enjoy hot.

SIMPLE
Cornstarch Gravy

Prep Time: 2 mins
Total Time: 10 mins

Servings per Recipe: 1
Calories	233.5 kcal
Fat	14.2 g
Cholesterol	7.2 mg
Sodium	477.2 mg
Carbohydrates	19.5 g
Protein	6.2 g

Ingredients

2 tbsp margarine
3 tbsp cornstarch
2 C. chicken stock

Directions

1. In a pot, add the butter over medium-high heat and cook until melted.
2. Add the cornstarch, beating continuously until smooth.
3. Cook for about 1 minute.
4. Slowly, add the stock, beating continuously until smooth.
5. Set the heat to medium and cook until desired thickness, mixing continuously.
6. Stir in the thyme, salt and pepper and enjoy hot..

Beef Broth Based Gravy

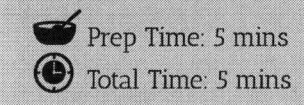

🥣 Prep Time: 5 mins
🕐 Total Time: 5 mins

Servings per Recipe: 4
Calories	108.6 kcal
Fat	8.7 g
Cholesterol	22.9 mg
Sodium	576.1 mg
Carbohydrates	5.4 g
Protein	2.5 g

Ingredients

3 tbsp butter
3 tbsp all-purpose flour
1 (10 1/2 oz.) cans campbells condensed beef broth
1 -2 tsp Worcestershire sauce
1/4-1/2 tsp garlic powder
1/4 tsp ground pepper

Directions

1. In a pot, add the butter over medium heat and cook until melted.
2. Add the flour, beating continuously until well combined.
3. Gradually, add the broth, beating continuously.
4. Stir in the Worcestershire sauce, garlic powder and pepper AND cook until desired thickness of the gravy.
5. Enjoy hot.

DAIRY-FREE
Gravy

🥣 Prep Time: 10 mins
🕐 Total Time: 25 mins

Servings per Recipe: 4
Calories   132.6 kcal
Fat   0.9 g
Cholesterol   0.0 mg
Sodium   3730.4mg
Carbohydrates   20.4 g
Protein   13.1 g

Ingredients

- 6 button mushrooms, chopped
- 2 tbsp vegan margarine
- 3 tbsp flour
- 1 tbsp nutritional yeast
- 1/4 tsp black pepper
- 1 tsp tamari
- 1 C. vegetable stock

Directions

1. In a skillet, melt the margarine over medium-high heat and cook the mushrooms for about 6-7 minutes.
2. Add the nutritional yeast, flour, pepper and tamari and cook until desired thickness, mixing continuously.
3. Remove from the heat and with an immersion blender, blend the gravy until smooth.
4. Enjoy hot.

Mexican
Masa Harina Gravy

🥣 Prep Time: 10 mins
🕐 Total Time: 50 mins

Servings per Recipe: 2
Calories	231.5 kcal
Fat	19.6 g
Cholesterol	3.0 mg
Sodium	1165.0 mg
Carbohydrates	12.7 g
Protein	5.5 g

Ingredients

- 4 tbsp peanut oil
- 1 medium onion, chopped
- 2 large garlic cloves, minced (
- 1 tbsp bacon drippings
- 1/2 C. chili powder
- 1/4 tsp ground cumin
- 1/4 tsp dried oregano
- 4 C. beef stock
- 1 tbsp masa harina
- salt

Directions

1. In a pan, heat the oil over medium heat and stir fry the onion and garlic for about 4-5 minutes.
2. Add the bacon drippings, oregano, cumin and chili powder, cumin and stir to combine.
3. Slowly, add the beef stock, mixing until well combined.
4. Set the heat to low and cook for about 30 minutes.
5. In a bowl, add the Masa Harina and a few tbsp of the water and mix well.
6. Stir the Masa Harina mixture into the gravy and cook for about 9-10 minutes.
7. Enjoy hot.

GRAVY
Rustica

Prep Time: 10 mins
Total Time: 10 mins

Servings per Recipe: 3
Calories			96.7 kcal
Fat				4.5 g
Cholesterol		17.0 mg
Sodium			447.5 mg
Carbohydrates	9.6 g
Protein			4.5 g

Ingredients

2 tbsp chicken drippings
2 tbsp all-purpose flour
1/2 tsp salt
1/4 tsp ground black pepper
1 1/2 C. milk

Directions

1. In the pot of the chicken drippings, add the flour over medium heat and cook until browned, stirring continuously.
2. Stir in the milk, salt and pepper and cook until boiling.
3. Cook for about 2 minutes, mixing continuously.
4. Enjoy hot..

Rojo Gravy over Burritos

Prep Time: 25 mins
Total Time: 11 hr 40 mins

Servings per Recipe: 10
Calories	362.4 kcal
Fat	7.6 g
Cholesterol	0.0 mg
Sodium	506.3 mg
Carbohydrates	60.3 g
Protein	14.9 g

Ingredients

Filling
- 2 1/2 C. dried pinto beans
- 6 C. water
- 2 onions, diced
- 1 pinch salt
- 2 jalapeño peppers, minced
- 6 medium garlic cloves, minced
- 1/2-3/4 C. onion, chopped
- 3 tsp ground cumin
- 2 tsp chili powder
- 2 tsp dried oregano
- 1 tsp sea salt
- 2 C. corn kernels
- 10 flour tortillas
- 1 green onion, sliced

Gravy
- 2 tsp minced chili peppers
- 1/4 tsp paprika
- 1/2 tsp salt
- 1 tbsp dried oregano
- 1/2 tsp cayenne pepper
- 2 tbsp chopped cilantro
- 1/4 onion, chopped
- 1 garlic clove, chopped
- 1/2 C. tomato sauce
- 2 C. water
- 3 tbsp flour
- 3 tbsp olive oil
- salt

Directions

1. For the bean filling: in a pan, add the beans and enough water to cover.
2. Keep aside overnight.
3. Drain the beans and then, rinse them well.
4. In the pot, add the beans, onions, pinch of salt and 6 C. of the water over high heat and cook until boiling.
5. Set the heat to low and cook, covered for about 3 hours.
6. Drain the beans well and with a potato masher, mash them well.
7. Add corn kernels, onion, garlic, jalapeño, spices and salt and mix well.
8. For the gravy: in a pot, add the onion, garlic, cilantro, chili pepper, tomato sauce, spices

and water and cook until boiling.
9. set the heat to low and cook for about 5 minutes.
10. Meanwhile, in a small bowl, add the olive oil and flour and mix until smooth.
11. Gradually, add the oil mixture into the pan, stirring continuously and cook until boiling.
12. Cook until desired thickness of the gravy, mixing frequently.
13. Place the tortillas over a hot burner, one at a time until warmed through.
14. Place the beans mixture in the center of each tortilla and roll like a burrito.
15. Divide the tortillas onto serving plates and top with the gravy.
16. Enjoy with a garnishing of the green onions.

Herbed Gravy

Prep Time: 5 mins
Total Time: 20 mins

Servings per Recipe: 6
Calories   208.3 kcal
Fat   13.6 g
Cholesterol   0.0 mg
Sodium   877.9 mg
Carbohydrates   16.3 g
Protein   9.3 g

Ingredients

- 1/2 C. nutritional yeast
- 1/2 C. whole wheat flour
- 1/3 C. canola oil
- 1/2 C. chopped onion
- 2 tsp minced garlic
- 2 tsp chopped thyme
- 2 tsp chopped sage
- 4 C. water
- 1/4 C. tamari
- 1/2 tsp sea salt
- 1/2 tsp ground black pepper

Directions

1. In a wok, add the flour and nutritional year and flour over medium heat and cook for about 4 minutes, stirring continuously.
2. Remove from the heat and keep aside.
3. In a Heavy-bottomed pan, add the oil over medium heat and cook until heated.
4. Add the onion and cook for about 10 minutes, stirring frequently.
5. Stir in the garlic, sage and thyme and stir fry for about 40 seconds.
6. Add the flour mixture, beating continuously until well combined.
7. Stir in the tamari, salt, pepper and water and cook until boiling, mixing frequently.
8. Cook until desired thickness of the sauce.
9. Enjoy hot

CAROLINA
Gravy with Handmade Buttermilk Biscuits

Prep Time: 15 mins
Total Time: 45 mins

Servings per Recipe: 6
Calories	506.4 kcal
Fat	29.5 g
Cholesterol	13.0 mg
Sodium	1607.9 mg
Carbohydrates	50.2 g
Protein	9.9 g

Ingredients

- 2 1/2 C. self-rising flour
- 1/2 C. vegetable shortening
- 1 C. buttermilk
- Gravy
- 4 tbsp vegetable shortening
- 1/3 C. self-rising flour
- 2 C. milk
- 2 tsp salt
- 1 tbsp ground black pepper

Directions

1. Set your oven to 425 degrees F before doing anything else.
2. In a bowl, place the flour.
3. With a pastry blender, cut in the shortening until a coarse crumb like mixture is formed.
4. Add the buttermilk and mix until a soft dough is formed.
5. Place the dough onto a generously floured board and roll into a ball.
6. With your hands, knead for about 5 minutes.
7. Now, with your hands, pat the dough into 1/3-inch thickness.
8. With a 1 1/2-2-inch round biscuit cutter, cut the biscuits from the dough.
9. Arrange the biscuits onto an ungreased cookie sheet in a single layer about 1-inch apart.
10. Cook in the oven for about 15-20 minutes.
11. For the gravy: in a wok, add the shortening and cook until melted.
12. Stir in the flour until smooth.
13. Add 1/2 C. of the milk, stirring continuously until smooth.
14. Add the remaining milk, mixing continuously until smooth.
15. Stir in the salt and pepper and remove from the heat.
16. Keep aside for about 6 minutes.
17. Enjoy the biscuits alongside the gravy.

10-Minute Gravy

🥣 Prep Time: 2 mins
🕐 Total Time: 10 mins

Servings per Recipe: 1
Calories	559.1 kcal
Fat	56.3 g
Cholesterol	193.5 mg
Sodium	520.0 mg
Carbohydrates	9.5 g
Protein	5.8 g

Ingredients

2 tbsp butter
2 tbsp all-purpose flour
1 C. heavy cream
1 C. chicken broth
kosher salt, ground black pepper
lemon juice, a squeeze

Directions

1. In a microwave-safe bowl, add the butter and microwave on power for about 2 minutes.
2. Remove from the microwave and add the flour, beating continuously.
3. Now, microwave on power for about 2 minutes.
4. Remove from the microwave and add the cream and broth, beating continuously.
5. Now, microwave on power for about 2 minutes.
6. Enjoy hot.

SWEET Roasted Turkey with Gravy

🥣 Prep Time: 4 hrs
⏱ Total Time: 8 hrs

Servings per Recipe: 12
Calories   1511.2 kcal
Fat   77.7 g
Cholesterol   575.8 mg
Sodium   844.3 mg
Carbohydrates   29.1 g
Protein   164.9 g

Ingredients

Glazed
1 C. apricot nectar
1 C. apricot preserves
2 tbsp minced peeled ginger
1 tbsp honey
Flavored Butter
3/4 C. unsalted butter
3 tbsp chopped thyme
3 tbsp chopped sage
1 1/2 tsp salt
1 tsp ground black pepper
Onion

2 tbsp unsalted butter
3 large onions, sliced
6 oz. shallots, sliced
Meat
21 - 22 lb. turkey, pat dried
1 (14 1/2 oz.) cans low sodium chicken broth
1 tsp chopped thyme
1/2 tsp chopped sage
Gravy
1 (14 1/2 oz.) cans low sodium chicken broth

Directions

1. For the apricot glaze: in a pot, add all the ingredients over high heat and cook until boiling.
2. Set the heat to medium-low and cook for about 13-15 minutes.
3. For the herb butter: in a bowl, add all the ingredients and mix until well combined.
4. For the onion mixture: in a wok, add the butter over medium heat and cook until melted.
5. Add the shallots and onions and cook for about 18-20 minutes, stirring frequently.
6. remove from the heat and transfer the onion mixture into a bowl.
7. Cover the bowl and refrigerate to chill.
8. For the turkey: set your oven to 400 degrees F and arrange a rack in the lowest third of oven. Arrange a wire rack in a roasting pan.

9. Rub the turkey cavity with salt and pepper evenly.
10. Arrange the turkey into the prepared roasting pan.
11. Carefully, loosen the skin under the turkey breast.
12. Place 1/2 of the herb butter under the skin of breast evenly.
13. In a frying pan, add the remaining herb butter over low heat and cook until melted completely.
14. Remove from the heat and keep aside to cool slightly.
15. Coat the outside of turkey with the melted herb butter.
16. With kitchen strings, tie the turkey legs together loosely.
17. Cook in the oven for about 30 minutes.
18. Now, set your oven to 325 degrees F.
19. Cook for about 1 1/2 hours, coating with the pan drippings time by time.
20. Now, cover the turkey with a piece of the foil and cook for about 45 minutes.
21. In the roasting pan, add the onion mixture, sage, thyme and 1 can of the broth.
22. Cook for about 15 minutes.
23. Place the pan of the glaze over heat and cook until just boiling.
24. Now, coat the turkey with 1/2 C. of the glaze evenly and cook for about 40 minutes,
25. coating with the glaze often. (You can add more broth in roasting pan if required).
26. Remove the turkey from the oven, reserving pan juices for gravy.
27. Transfer the turkey onto a platter and with a piece of foil; cover it for about 30 minutes.
28. For the gravy: through a strainer, strain the pan mixture into a bowl, reserving solids
29. With a slotted spoon, remove the fat from the pan juices.
30. In a blender, add the reserved solids and
31. 1 C. of the pan juices and pulse until smooth.
32. In a heavy bottomed pan, add the pureed mixture and cook until boiling.
33. Cook for about 5 minutes, removing the foam from top.
34. Stir in the salt and pepper and remove from the heat.
35. Enjoy the turkey alongside the gravy..

AMISH
Friendship Gravy

Prep Time: 10 mins
Total Time: 30 mins

Servings per Recipe: 4
Calories	101.5 kcal
Fat	6.4 g
Cholesterol	7.7 mg
Sodium	254.9 mg
Carbohydrates	9.3 g
Protein	1.4 g

Ingredients

3 C. hot broth
3/4 C. flour
1/8 tsp garlic powder
1/8 tsp onion powder
1/8 tsp white pepper
2 tbsp butter

2 tbsp peanut oil
salt

Directions

1. In a wok, add the peanut oil and butter over low heat and cook until heated completely.
2. Stir in the flour and cook until aromatic, stirring continuously.
3. Gradually, add the broth, beating continuously until smooth.
4. Stir in the spices and cook for about 18-20 minutes, mixing occasionally.
5. Enjoy hot..

2-Ingredient Tangy Gravy

🍲 Prep Time: 5 mins
🕐 Total Time: 10 mins

Servings per Recipe: 6
Calories   275.4 kcal
Fat   30.6 g
Cholesterol   81.3 mg
Sodium   218.9 mg
Carbohydrates   0.2 g
Protein   0.3 g

Ingredients

1/2 lb. butter
1/2 C. cider vinegar

Directions

1. In a pot, add the butter and cook until butter becomes medium dark brown, stirring continuously.
2. Stir in the vinegar and remove from the heat.
3. Enjoy hot.

SPOKANE
Nutty Gravy

Prep Time: 10 mins
Total Time: 25 mins

Servings per Recipe: 1
Calories   8.0 kcal
Fat   0.0 g
Cholesterol   0.0 mg
Sodium   406.6 mg
Carbohydrates   1.1 g
Protein   1.0 g

Ingredients

- 4 C. water
- 2 tbsp onions, chopped
- 1/4 tsp granulated garlic
- 2 tbsp Braggs liquid aminos
- 2 tbsp tamari soy sauce
- 1/2 C. mushrooms, chopped
- 1/2 C. walnuts, chopped
- 3 1/2 tbsp cornstarch mixed in with water

Directions

1. In a pot, add the onions, mushrooms, garlic, walnuts, tamari, liquid aminos and water and cook until boiling.
2. Now, set the heat to low.
3. Gradually, add the cornstarch mixture, beating continuously until smooth.
4. Cook for about 10 minutes, mixing frequently.
5. Enjoy hot..

Gravy Skillet

Prep Time: 1 mins
Total Time: 6 mins

Servings per Recipe: 8
Calories	56.9 kcal
Fat	4.2 g
Cholesterol	12.9 mg
Sodium	44.0 mg
Carbohydrates	3.2 g
Protein	1.4 g

Ingredients

- 2 tbsp butter
- 2 tbsp flour
- 1 1/4 C. milk
- salt
- pepper

Directions

1. In a skillet, melt the butter over low heat.
2. Add the flour, stirring continuously until smooth.
3. Slowly, add the milk, beating continuously and then, cook until desired thickness.

ARKANSAS
Fried Chicken

Prep Time: 5 mins
Total Time: 20 mins

Servings per Recipe: 2
Calories   876.6 kcal
Fat   62.8 g
Cholesterol   142.1 mg
Sodium   853.7 mg
Carbohydrates   33.6 g
Protein   44.0 g

Ingredients

2 chicken breasts
1 (12 oz.) cans evaporated milk
1 tsp lemon juice
1/3 C. flour
1/2 tsp salt
1/2 tsp black pepper
1/4 tsp cayenne pepper
1/3 C. vegetable oil

Directions

1. In a shallow dish, add the lemon juice and milk and mix.
2. In a separate shallow dish, add the flour, cayenne, salt and pepper and mix well.
3. Coat the chicken breasts with the milk mixture and then with the flour mixture.
4. Reserve the remaining milk and flour mixture.
5. In a wok, add the oil over medium-high heat and cook until heated.
6. Add the chicken and cook for about 4-6 minutes per side.
7. Transfer the chicken into a bowl.
8. In the same wok, add the reserved flour mixture over medium-high heat and stir fry for about 1 minute.
9. Slowly, add the reserved milk mixture, beating continuously.
10. Cook for about 2-3 minutes, beating continuously.
11. Enjoy the chicken with a topping of the gravy..

Guyanese Jumbo Shrimp with Gravy

Prep Time: 10 mins
Total Time: 15 mins

Servings per Recipe: 2
Calories	336.7 kcal
Fat	30.0 g
Cholesterol	105.8 mg
Sodium	499.8 mg
Carbohydrates	6.2 g
Protein	14.3 g

Ingredients

6 uncooked jumbo shrimp, deveined and unpeeled
1/4 tsp chili powder
1/4 tsp turmeric powder
1/4 tsp coriander powder
1/4 tsp cumin powder
1/4 tsp garam masala powder
8 fluid oz. coconut milk
1/2 C. cilantro leaf, chopped
3 garlic cloves, grated
1/2 tbsp vegetable oil
salt

Directions

1. In a pan, add the oil and cook until heated.
2. Add the cilantro, garlic and spices and stir to combine.
3. Stir in the shrimp and cook until opaque.
4. Stir in the coconut milk and salt and cook until boiling.
5. Cook until desired thickness.
6. Enjoy hot.

TALLAHASSEE
Country Gravy

Prep Time: 5 mins
Total Time: 15 mins

Servings per Recipe: 8
Calories   25.3 kcal
Fat   0.3 g
Cholesterol   0.0 mg
Sodium   143.4 mg
Carbohydrates   4.0 g
Protein   1.3 g

Ingredients

1/2 C. dripping, from the pan
1 1/2 C. chicken broth
1/4 C. flour
1/4 C. orange juice
2 tsp parsley, chopped
1 1/2 tsp chopped rosemary

1/2 tsp orange zest

Directions

1. After cooking of the turkey in oven, remove the bird from the roasting pan.
2. With a slotted spoon, remove the fat from the top, leaving about 1/2 C. of the drippings inside.
3. In a bowl, add the flour and broth and stir until well combined.
4. Add the flour mixture into the roasting pan with the drippings and mix well.
5. Stir in the parsley, rosemary, orange zest and orange juice
6. Place the roasting pan over medium heat and cook until desired thickness.
7. Enjoy hot..

Marjoram Wheat Gravy

🍲 Prep Time: 12 mins
🕐 Total Time: 1 hr 2 mins

Servings per Recipe: 6
Calories   83.6 kcal
Fat   4.7 g
Cholesterol   0.0 mg
Sodium   227.2 mg
Carbohydrates   9.0 g
Protein   2.1 g

Ingredients

- 1 head garlic
- 6 tbsp whole wheat pastry flour
- 1 tbsp olive oil
- 1 tbsp canola oil
- 2 C. water
- 4 -6 tsp soy sauce
- 1 tsp dried thyme leaves, crumbled
- 1 tsp dried marjoram

Directions

1. Set your oven to 350 degrees F before doing anything else.
2. In a baking dish, add the garlic and top with about 2-inch of water.
3. Cook in the oven for about 25-30 minutes.
4. Remove the roasted garlic from oven and keep aside to cool.
5. Carefully, remove the top of garlic head.
6. Remove the skin of garlic cloves and place into a bowl, discarding the skin.
7. With a fork, mash the garlic cloves.
8. In a pan, add the flour over medium heat and cook until fragrant, mixing continuously.
9. Add the oil, beating strenuously until well combined.
10. Set the heat to low and stir in the garlic.
11. Cook for about 2 minutes, mixing occasionally.
12. Stir in the herbs, soy sauce and water and cook for about 18-20 minutes, mixing often.
13. Enjoy hot.

GRAVY
Spice Mix for Gravies

Prep Time: 10 mins
Total Time: 2 hrs 10 mins

Servings per Recipe: 1
Calories   233.7 kcal
Fat   0.8 g
Cholesterol   0.0 mg
Sodium   583.4 mg
Carbohydrates   49.0 g
Protein   6.7 g

Ingredients

1 C. all-purpose flour
2 tsp garlic salt
1 tsp paprika
1 tsp ground black pepper
1/4 tsp poultry seasoning
1/2 tsp salt

Directions

1. For the gravy mix in a bowl, add all the ingredients and mix until well combined.
2. Transfer into an airtight container to store.
3. For the gravy: in a wok, add 2 tbsp of the unsalted butter over low heat and cook until melted.
4. Stir in 2 tbsp of the gravy mix and cook for about 2 minutes, mixing continuously.
5. Add 1 C. of the chicken broth, stirring continuously.
6. Add 1 C. of the milk and stir to combine.
7. Increase the heat to high, mixing continuously.
8. Set the heat to low and cook for about 4-5 minutes.
9. Enjoy hot..

Beef Croquettes with Curry Paste Gravy

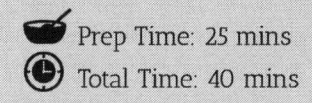

Prep Time: 25 mins
Total Time: 40 mins

Servings per Recipe: 4
Calories   636.4 kcal
Fat   35.8 g
Cholesterol   102.9 mg
Sodium   178.2 mg
Carbohydrates   48.5 g
Protein   30.8 g

Ingredients

vegetable oil
2 spring onions, chopped
4 garlic cloves
600 g minced beef
1 tbsp Greek yogurt
1 tsp garam masala
1 -2 tsp curry paste
ground salt
ground pepper
plain flour
cooking spray

1 brown onion, wedges)
2 tbsp curry paste
6 cardamom pods, crushed
1/2 stick cinnamon
3 whole cloves
2 bay leaves
1 - 1 1/2 C. coconut cream
1/2 C. tomatoes diced
1/2-1 C. chicken stock
steamed rice

Directions

1. Set your oven to 350 degrees F and lightly, grease 1-2 baking sheets.
2. Grease a pan with vegetable oil slightly and heat it.
3. Add 2 minced garlic cloves and spring onion and stir fry for about 3 minutes.
4. Remove from the heat.
5. Add the beef, 2 tbsp of the coriander, yoghurt, chili paste, garam masala and seasonings and mix until well combined.
6. Make 8 equal sized rissoles from the mixture.
7. Coat the rissoles with flour evenly.
8. Arrange the rissoles onto the prepared baking sheets in a single layer.
9. Cook in the oven for about 15 minutes, flipping once after 7 minutes.
10. Remove from the oven and drain the grease from baking sheets completely.
11. Meanwhile, grease a frying pan with vegetable oil slightly and heat it.

12. Add the brown onion and 2 sliced garlic cloves and stir fry
13. Add the curry paste with the cardamom, cinnamon, cloves and bay leaves and mix well and briefly cook to toast the spices. and then add about 1 C. coconut cream with the tomatoes, 1/2 C. stock and seasonings and cook for about 5 minutes until reduced quite heavily, adding more coconut cream and/or stock as needed, taste for seasoning.

Easy Egg Gravy

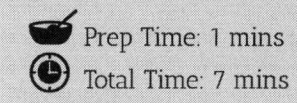

Prep Time: 1 mins
Total Time: 7 mins

Servings per Recipe: 2
Calories   264.4 kcal
Fat   21.7 g
Cholesterol   243.2 mg
Sodium   169.3 mg
Carbohydrates   7.5 g
Protein   9.7 g

Ingredients

2 large eggs
1 tbsp butter
1 tbsp flour
1/4 C. whipping cream, liquid
1/2 C. skim milk
seasoned salt,
black pepper

Directions

1. In a skillet, break both and cook until eggs are set slightly.
2. Stir in the salt and pepper and remove from the heat.
3. With a slotted spoon, transfer the eggs into a bowl.
4. In the same skillet, add the butter over medium-low heat and cook until melted.
5. Slowly, add the flour and stir until well combined.
6. Slowly, add the whipping cream and stir until well combined.
7. Add the skim milk, a little at a time and stir to combine well.
8. Se the heat to medium-low and cook until just boiling.
9. Cook until gravy becomes thick.
10. Chop the eggs and stir into gravy.
11. Remove from the heat and enjoy.

HOW to Make Glazed Lamb Chops

Prep Time: 30 mins
Total Time: 1 hr

Servings per Recipe: 6
Calories   881.9 kcall
Fat   58.9 g
Cholesterol   152.0 mg
Sodium   809.7 mg
Carbohydrates   43.9 g
Protein   41.0 g

Ingredients

Gravy
3 tbsp all-purpose flour
2 tbsp olive oil
2 C. whole milk
salt & ground black pepper
1 tsp sugar
Meat

oil
2 tsp kosher salt
1 tbsp ground black pepper
2 C. all-purpose flour
12 single-rib frenched lamb chops
2 C. buttermilk

Directions

1. For the gravy: in a pot, add the oil over medium heat and cook until just heated.
2. Stir in the flour and cook for about 11-12 minutes, beating continuously.
3. until a peanut-brown color.
4. Stir in the milk, sugar, salt and pepper and cook until boiling, , beating continuously
5. Set the heat to low heat and cook for about 12-15 minutes beating frequently.
6. For the lamb: in a shallow dish, add the flour, salt and pepper and mix well.
7. In another shallow dish, place the buttermilk.
8. Coat the lamb chops evenly with the flour mixture and then, dip into buttermilk and finally again coat with the flour mixture.
9. In a skillet, heat about 1-inch deep oil until its temperature reaches to 365 degrees F
10. Add the lamb chops in batches and cook for 2-3 minutes on both sides.
11. With a slotted spoon, transfer the lambs onto paper towel-lined plate to drain.
12. Enjoy the chops alongside the gravy..

Alabama Gravy for Biscuits

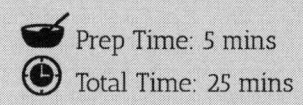

🥣 Prep Time: 5 mins
🕐 Total Time: 25 mins

Servings per Recipe: 6
Calories	215.8 kcal
Fat	10.7 g
Cholesterol	47.9 mg
Sodium	202.2 mg
Carbohydrates	12.4 g
Protein	16.2 g

Ingredients

Meat Base
8 oz. lean ground beef
1/4 tsp ground black pepper
1/2 tsp seasoning salt
1 tsp sausage seasoning
Sauce
2 1/2 C. skim milk

1/4 C. all-purpose flour
8 oz. reduced-fat cream cheese, chunks
1/2 tsp Worcestershire sauce
2-3 drops hot sauce

Directions

1. Heat a wok over medium heat and cook the crumbled beef with the sausage seasoning, half of the salt and black pepper until browned completely.
2. Meanwhile, in a bowl, add the milk and flour and mix well and keep aside.
3. Drain the fat from the beef completely.
4. Add the milk mixture and stir to combine.
5. Stir in the cheese and set the heat to medium low.
6. Cook for about 10 minutes, mixing occasionally.
7. Stir in the Worcestershire sauce and Tabasco sauce and set the heat to low.
8. Cook until desired thickness of the gravy.
9. Enjoy hot.

CHICAGO
Top Roast with Spicy Gravy

🥣 Prep Time: 10 mins
🕒 Total Time: 8 hrs 20 mins

Servings per Recipe: 8
Calories 423.5 kcal
Fat 20.3 g
Cholesterol 156.4 mg
Sodium 284.4 mg
Carbohydrates 6.1 g
Protein 50.6 g

Ingredients

4 lb. beef top round roast, trimmed of fat
1/2 tsp sea salt
1/4 tsp ground black pepper
4 tsp olive oil, divided
2 large onions halved and sliced
4 Serrano peppers, whole, seeds removed
4 garlic cloves, minced
1 tbsp thyme, chopped
1/2 C. strong brewed coffee
2 tbsp red wine vinegar
2 tbsp cornstarch
2 tbsp water

Directions

1. Season the beef roast with the salt and pepper evenly.
2. In a pan, add 2 tsp of the oil over medium heat and cook until heated.
3. Add the beef roast and sear for about 8-10 minutes.
4. Place the roast into the crock pot.
5. In the same pan, heat 2 tsp of the oil and stir fry the onions for about 6-7 minutes.
6. Add the Serrano peppers, thyme and garlic and stir fry for about 1 minute.
7. Stir in the vinegar and coffee and; cook until boiling.
8. Place the onion mixture over the roast into crock pot.
9. Set the crock pot on High and cook, covered for about 4 1/2-5 hours.
10. Uncover the crock pot and place the roast onto a cutting board.
11. With a piece of the foil, cover the roast for about 9-10 minutes.
12. Transfer the cooking liquid into a pot.
13. With a slotted spoon, remove the fat from the top of the cooking liquid.
14. Place the pot over medium heat and cook until boiling.
15. Meanwhile, in a bowl, dissolve the cornstarch into the water.
16. Add the cornstarch mixture into the pot, stirring continuously.

17. Cook for about 1-2 minute, stirring continuously.
18. Stir in the black pepper and remove from the heat.
19. Discard the Serrano peppers.
20. Cut the roast into desired sized slices and enjoy alongside the gravy..

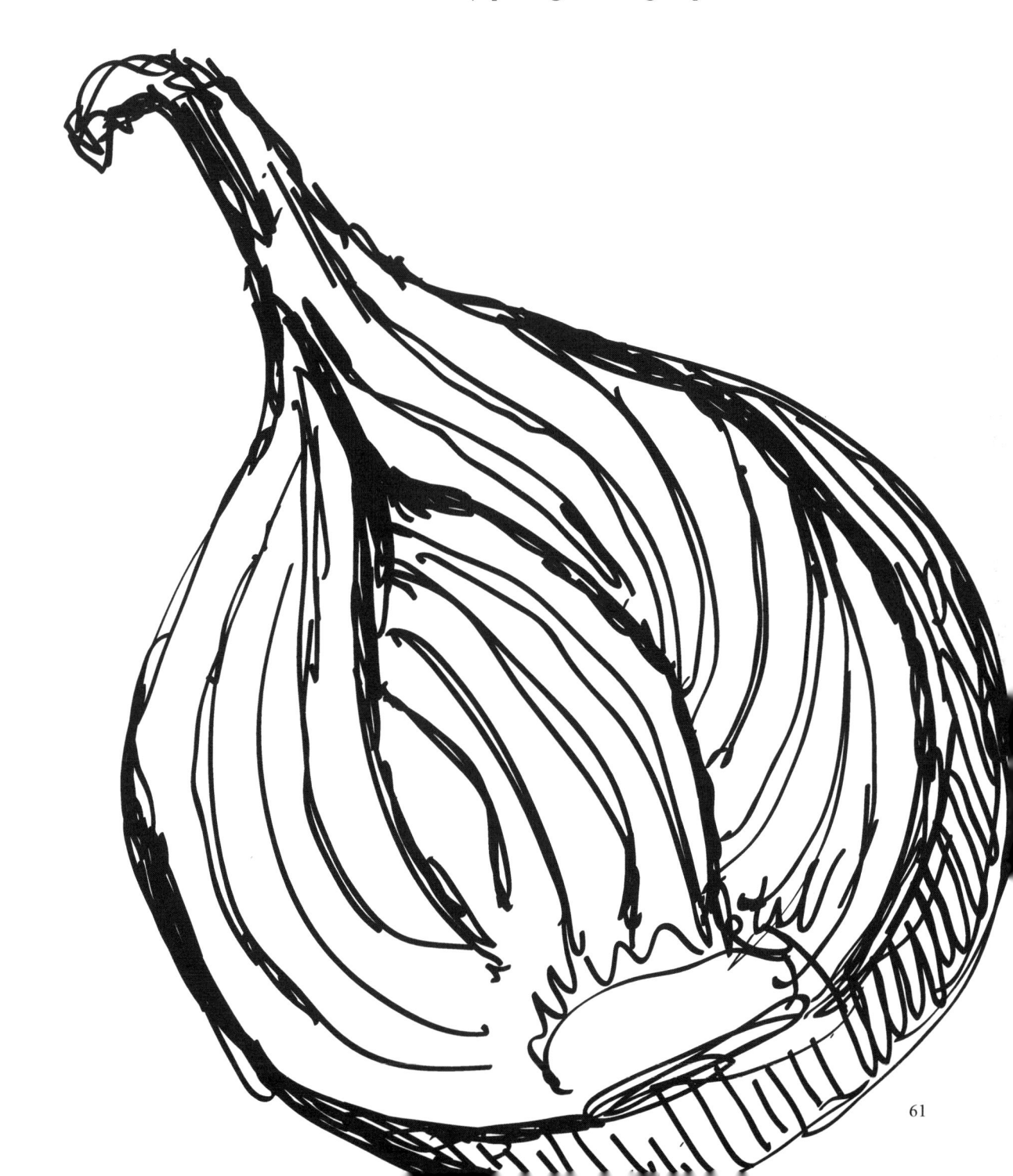

TURKEY Burgers with Gravy

Prep Time: 30 mins
Total Time: 30 mins

Servings per Recipe: 6
Calories   560.4 kcal
Fat   23.9 g
Cholesterol   143.0 mg
Sodium   744.0 mg
Carbohydrates   33.3 g
Protein   50.9 g

Ingredients

Burgers
2 lb. lean ground turkey breast
2 - 4 tbsp grill seasoning
1/4 C. buffalo wing sauce
1/4 C. chives, chopped
1/4 C. parsley, chopped
2 garlic cloves, grated
2 tbsp olive oil
Gravy
3 tbsp butter

3 tbsp flour
3 C. milk
1 C. blue cheese
salt
ground pepper,
Toppings
3 carrots, peeled and cut into sticks
3 stalks celery, cut into sticks
4 Kaiser rolls

Directions

1. In a bowl, add the turkey, garlic, parsley, chives, grill seasoning and hot sauce and mix until well combined.
2. Make 6 equal sized patties from the mixture.
3. In a skillet, 2 tbsp of the oil over medium-high heat and cook until heated.
4. Add the burgers and cook for about 5 minutes per side.
5. Meanwhile, in another skillet, add the butter over medium-high heat and cook until melted.
6. Add the flour and cook for about 1 minute, stirring continuously.
7. Slowly, add the milk beating continuously.
8. Stir in the salt and black pepper and cook until just boiling.
9. Remove from the heat and stir in the blue cheese until smooth.
10. Arrange the top of the roll onto a plate and top with the burger.
11. Enjoy the burgers with a garnishing of the chives alongside the carrot, celery sticks and warm blue cheese gravy..

Kentucky
Liver and Onions

Prep Time: 2 hrs
Total Time: 2 hrs

Servings per Recipe: 4
Calories	421.0 kcal
Fat	23.5 g
Cholesterol	370. 7 mg
Sodium	452.6 mg
Carbohydrates	19.4 g
Protein	32.3 g

Ingredients

- 1 lb. beef liver, rinsed and dried
- 2 C. milk
- 1 C. beef broth
- 1/2 C. mozzarella cheese, shredded
- 4 tbsp butter
- 4 tbsp gluten-free all-purpose flour
- 1 medium onion, halved and sliced
- 1 C. mushroom, quartered

Directions

1. In a bowl, place the liver and top with 1 C. of the milk.
2. Place in the fridge for about 1 1/2-2 hours.
3. Drain the liver, discarding the milk.
4. Then, cut the liver into 1-inch cubes.
5. Heat a nonstick skillet over medium heat and stir fry the liver until golden brown.
6. Transfer the liver onto a plate and keep aside.
7. In the same skillet, add the mushrooms and onions and cook for about 6-7 minutes.
8. Transfer the mushroom mixture onto the plate and keep aside.
9. In the same skillet, add the butter and cook until melted.
10. Stir in the flour and cook for about 1-2 minutes, stirring continuously.
11. Add the milk and broth over medium-high heat and cook until sauce just starts to become thick, stirring frequently.
12. Slowly, add the cheese, mixing continuously until melted completely.
13. Stir in the cooked liver and mushroom mixture and cook until heated completely.
14. Stir in the salt and pepper and remove from the heat.
15. Enjoy hot.

AMERICAN
Cornstarch Gravy

Prep Time: 5 mins
Total Time: 20 mins

Servings per Recipe: 1
Calories	383.1 kcal
Fat	23.5 g
Cholesterol	0.0 mg
Sodium	2286.9 mg
Carbohydrates	34.7 g
Protein	11.2 g

Ingredients

2 tbsp margarine
1 diced onion
2 tbsp flour
1 tsp garlic salt
2 tsp cornstarch
1 1/2 C. vegetable broth

2 tbsp soy sauce
1 tbsp nutritional yeast

Directions

1. In a wok, add the margarine over medium heat and cook until melted.
2. Add the onion and stir fry for bout 2-3 minutes.
3. Stir in the flour and garlic salt and stir fry for about 7-10 minutes.
4. Stir in the cornstarch and broth and cook until boiling, stirring frequently.
5. Set the heat to low and stir in the soy sauce and nutritional yeast.
6. Cook until desired thickness of the gravy.
7. Enjoy hot..

Spicy Tomato Gravy from Ghana

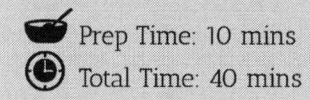

Prep Time: 10 mins
Total Time: 40 mins

Servings per Recipe: 4
Calories	309.7 kcal
Fat	27.8 g
Cholesterol	0.0 mg
Sodium	14.0 mg
Carbohydrates	15.4 g
Protein	2.7 g

Ingredients

2 medium onions, diced
8 Roma tomatoes
1/2 C. vegetable oil
1 tsp cayenne pepper
1 tsp seasoning salt
1/2 tsp thyme
1 green pepper, diced

Directions

1. In a skillet, add the oil and cook until heated.
2. Add the onions and stir fry for about 5-6 minutes.
3. Add the tomatoes, green pepper, thyme, seasoning salt and cayenne pepper and cook for about 28-30 minutes.
4. Enjoy hot.

5-INGREDIENT
Garlicky Gravy

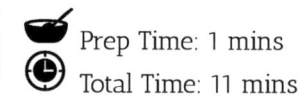

Prep Time: 1 mins
Total Time: 11 mins

Servings per Recipe: 4
Calories   149.8 kcal
Fat   11.1 g
Cholesterol   8.5 mg
Sodium   320.8 mg
Carbohydrates   8.4 g
Protein   4.1 g

Ingredients

3 tbsp margarine
3 tbsp all-purpose flour
1 C. milk
1 C. chicken broth
2 tsp garlic powder

Directions

1. In a wok, add the butter over medium heat and cook until melted.
2. Add the flour, stirring continuously until melted completely.
3. Add the broth and milk and beat until smooth.
4. Add the garlic powder and stir to combine.
5. Set the heat to low and cook for about 4-5 minutes.
6. Enjoy hot..

Mexi-Cajun Steak with Gravy

🍲 Prep Time: 20 mins
⏱ Total Time: 35 mins

Servings per Recipe: 4
Calories   567.9 kcal
Fat   39.3 g
Cholesterol   154.1 mg
Sodium   564.5 mg
Carbohydrates   9.0 g
Protein   42.9 g

Ingredients

4 (5 oz.) beef top sirloin steaks, rinsed and pat dried
Cajun seasoning
2 large poblano peppers
2 tbsp butter
2 tbsp flour
2 C. beef stock
2 tsp Worcestershire sauce
1 tsp ground cumin
salt and pepper

Directions

1. Set the broiler of your oven.
2. Cook the peppers under the broiler until the skin becomes blackened.
3. Remove the peppers from the oven and immediately, place into a paper bag.
4. Seal the bag and keep aside to cool.
5. Carefully, remove the skin of each pepper.
6. Cut each pepper in half and remove the seeds.
7. In a food processor, add the peppers and a little beef stock and pulse until smooth.
8. Now, place the steaks onto the broiler rack and cook under the broiler for about 6-8 minutes on both sides.
9. Remove from the oven and place the steak onto a cutting board for about 10 minutes before slicing.
10. In a pan, add the butter over medium low heat and cook until melted.
11. Stir in the flour and cook until flour becomes golden brown, stirring continuously.

12. Add the beef stock, cumin and Worcestershire sauce and cook until gravy becomes slightly thick.
13. Add the pureed peppers and cook until desired thickness of the gravy.
14. Stir in the salt and pepper and remove from the heat.
15. Cut the steak into 1/4-inch slices.
16. Enjoy the steak slices with a topping of the gravy.

Salisbury Steaks

Prep Time: 15 mins
Total Time: 45 mins

Servings per Recipe: 4
Calories	468.6 kcal
Fat	27.8 g
Cholesterol	135.8 mg
Sodium	1319.6 mg
Carbohydrates	23.8 g
Protein	30.4 g

Ingredients

- 1 lb. lean ground beef
- 1 (10 oz.) cans condensed cream of mushroom soup, divided
- 1/2 C. Italian seasoned breadcrumbs
- 1 egg, lightly beaten
- 1/2 C. chopped onion
- 1 tbsp steak seasoning
- 1 tbsp canola oil
- 2 tbsp butter, divided
- 1 (8 oz.) packages sliced mushrooms
- 2 C. low sodium beef broth
- 1 (1 1/4 oz.) packets brown gravy mix

Directions

1. In a bowl, add the beef, onions, 1/4 of the mushroom soup, egg, breadcrumbs and steak seasoning and mix until well combined.
2. Make 4 equal sized oval shaped patties from the mixture.
3. In a skillet, add the oil and 1 tbsp of the butter over medium-high heat and cook until heated.
4. Add the patties and cook until browned from both sides,
5. Place the patties onto a plate.
6. In the same skillet, melt the remaining butter.
7. Add the mushrooms and cook for about 6-8 minutes.
8. Meanwhile, in a bowl, add the gravy mix and beef stock and mix until smooth.
9. Add the remaining mushroom soup and stock mixture into mushrooms and stir to combine.
10. Place the cooked patties in skillet.
11. With a spoon, place the gravy over the patties and simmer, covered for about 22-25 minutes.
12. Enjoy hot.

ONION
Mushroom Gravy

Prep Time: 5 mins
Total Time: 10 mins

Servings per Recipe: 8
Calories	22.7 kcal
Fat	0.3 g
Cholesterol	0.0 mg
Sodium	187.9 mg
Carbohydrates	3.2 g
Protein	1.5 g

Ingredients

1/2 C. onion, chopped
1/2 C. mushroom, chopped
2 tbsp parsley, chopped
2 C. chicken broth, divided
2 tbsp cornstarch
1 pinch pepper

Directions

1. In a pot, heat 1/4 C. of the broth over medium heat and stir fry the mushroom, onion and parsley for about 6-8 minutes.
2. Meanwhile, in a bowl, dissolve the cornstarch and pepper into 1/2 C. of the broth.
3. Stir the cornstarch mixture and remaining broth into the pot and cook until boiling, mixing often.
4. Cook for about 2-3 minutes, mixing often.
5. Enjoy hot..

Onion Mushroom Gravy

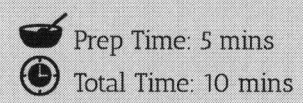

Prep Time: 5 mins
Total Time: 10 mins

Servings per Recipe: 8
Calories   22.7 kcal
Fat   0.3 g
Cholesterol   0.0 mg
Sodium   187.9 mg
Carbohydrates   3.2 g
Protein   1.5 g

Ingredients

- 1/2 C. onion, chopped
- 1/2 C. mushroom, chopped
- 2 tbsp parsley, chopped
- 2 C. chicken broth, divided
- 2 tbsp cornstarch
- 1 pinch pepper

Directions

1. In a pot, heat 1/4 C. of the broth over medium heat and stir fry the mushroom, onion and parsley for about 6-8 minutes.
2. Meanwhile, in a bowl, dissolve the cornstarch and pepper into 1/2 C. of the broth.
3. Stir the cornstarch mixture and remaining broth into the pot and cook until boiling, mixing often.
4. Cook for about 2-3 minutes, mixing often.
5. Enjoy hot.

FOOD Court Gravy

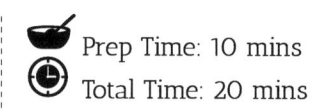

Prep Time: 10 mins
Total Time: 20 mins

Servings per Recipe: 6
Calories   92.3 kcal
Fat   7.1 g
Cholesterol   0.6 mg
Sodium   182.8 mg
Carbohydrates   5.8 g
Protein   1.3 g

Ingredients

- 2 C. cold filtered water
- 2/3 C. cold nonfat milk
- 1 1/2 tsp Kitchen Bouquet (browning sauce)
- 1 tsp Worcestershire sauce
- 1 drop sesame oil
- 1 1/2 tbsp cornstarch
- 2 tsp chicken bouillon powder
- 1 tsp onion powder
- 3/8 tsp paprika
- 3/8 tsp seasoning of your choice
- 1/4 tsp celery salt
- 1/4 tsp ground sage
- 1/4 tsp seasoning salt
- 1/8 tsp Accent seasoning
- 1 pinch ground thyme
- 3 tbsp vegetable shortening
- 2 tbsp all-purpose flour

Directions

1. In a bowl, add the water, milk, kitchen bouquet, and Worcestershire sauce and sesame oil and mix well.
2. In another bowl, add the cornstarch, bouillon powder, thyme and spices and mix well.
3. Add the cornstarch mixture into the milk mixture and mix until well combined.
4. In a pot, add the shortening over medium-low heat and cook until melted.
5. Stir in the flour and cook until just bubbly, stirring continuously.
6. Slowly, add the milk mixture, beating continuously until smooth.
7. Cook until boiling, beating continuously.
8. Set the heat to low and cook until desired thickness of the gravy, beating occasionally
9. Enjoy warm..

3-Ingredient Gravy

Prep Time: 2 mins
Total Time: 10 mins

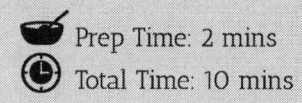

Servings per Recipe: 4
Calories	43.2 kcal
Fat	0.7 g
Cholesterol	0.0 mg
Sodium	36.6 mg
Carbohydrates	7.1 g
Protein	2.4 g

Ingredients

- 2 C. low sodium chicken broth
- 3 tbsp cornstarch
- 1 tsp poultry seasoning

Directions

1. In a pot, add the chicken stock and cook until boiling.
2. In a bowl add the cornstarch and a little water and mix until well combined.
3. Add the cornstarch mixture into the pot, stirring continuously.
4. Stir in the poultry seasoning and cook until desired thickness.
5. Enjoy hot.

RAW
Vegan Gravy

Prep Time: 10 mins
Total Time: 15 mins

Servings per Recipe: 5
Calories	88.6 kcal
Fat	6.3 g
Cholesterol	0.0 mg
Sodium	206.8 mg
Carbohydrates	6.3 g
Protein	2.7 g

Ingredients

2 C. water
1/2 C. raw cashews
1 tbsp unbleached white flour
1 tbsp vegan chicken seasoning
2 tsp onion powder
1/4 tsp celery salt
1 tbsp soy sauce
1 tsp dill
salt

Directions

1. In a food processor, add all the ingredients and pulse until smooth.
2. Transfer the pureed mixture into a pot over medium heat and cook until desired thickness.
3. Enjoy hot..

Shreveport Gravy

Prep Time: 5 mins
Total Time: 20 mins

Servings per Recipe: 4
Calories	454.9 kcal
Fat	22.8 g
Cholesterol	12.4 mg
Sodium	1290.5 mg
Carbohydrates	52.1 g
Protein	10.7 g

Ingredients

- 2 tbsp bacon grease, optional
- 2 tbsp flour
- 1 (16 oz.) cans tomatoes, diced
- 2 C. chicken stock
- 1 tsp salt
- 1 tsp pepper
- 6 biscuits

Directions

1. In a skillet, heat the bacon grease.
2. Add the flour, stirring continuously until smooth.
3. Stir in the salt and pepper.
4. Add the chicken stock, beating continuously until smooth.
5. Stir in the tomatoes and cook until desired thickness.
6. Enjoy hot.

CREAMY
Gouda Lunch Box

Prep Time: 5 mins
Total Time: 20 mins

Servings per Recipe: 4
Calories   350.2 kcal
Fat   10.0 g
Cholesterol   156.4 mg
Sodium   304.8 mg
Carbohydrates   4.8 g
Protein   56.6 g

Ingredients

4 skinless chicken breasts
2 tbsp thyme
salt and pepper
2 tbsp butter
2 tbsp flour
1/2 C. chicken broth

1/2 C. milk
1 C. gouda cheese, shredded

Directions

1. Season the chicken breasts with the thyme, salt and pepper evenly.
2. Heat a greased pan and cook the chicken for about 5-6 minute per side.
3. In another pan, add the butter and cook until melted.
4. Stir in the flour and cook for about 1-2 minutes, stirring continuously.
5. Add 1/2 C. of the milk and broth and cook for about 2-3 minute, stirring continuously.
6. Stir in the salt and pepper.
7. Add the cheese, stirring continuously until melted completely.
8. Remove from the heat.
9. Enjoy the chicken with a topping of the gravy..

Caribbean Gravy

🍲 Prep Time: 5 mins
🕐 Total Time: 1 hr 5 mins

Servings per Recipe: 4
Calories   14.2 kcal
Fat   0.1 g
Cholesterol   0.0 mg
Sodium   122.9 mg
Carbohydrates   2.8 g
Protein   0.6 g

Ingredients

2 tbsp whole wheat flour
1 C. fat free chicken broth
1/4 tsp poultry seasoning
salt and pepper
1/8-1/4 tsp Kitchen Bouquet (browning sauce)
Alternative Gravy

1/4 C. sliced mushrooms
For Dressing
1 C. fat free chicken broth
1 egg white

Directions

1. Place a heavy-bottomed wok over low heat until heated.
2. Stir in the flour and cook until golden brown, mixing continuously.
3. After cooking of the meat in oven, place the meat onto a platter.
4. With a slotted spoon, remove the fat from the top of the pan drippings.
5. In a bowl, add the browned flour and 1/2 of the pan drippings and mix well.
6. In a pan, add the flour mixture and remaining pan drippings and cook until boiling.
7. Cook until desired thickness of the gravy, mixing continuously.
8. Stir in the kitchen bouquet, salt and pepper and remove from the heat.

ROCKY Mount Bean Gravy

Prep Time: 5 mins
Total Time: 15 mins

Servings per Recipe: 8
Calories 127.5 kcal
Fat 2.1 g
Cholesterol 0.0 mg
Sodium 503.8 mg
Carbohydrates 21.5 g
Protein 6.0 g

Ingredients

1 tbsp olive oil
1 small onion, chopped
2 garlic cloves, chopped
3 tbsp thyme, chopped
pepper
1 1/2 C. vegetable broth
1/2 C. all-purpose flour
1 (15 oz.) cans navy beans, drained and rinsed
3 tbsp soy sauce
1/4 C. water
salt

Directions

1. In a pot, heat the oil over medium heat and stir fry the onion and garlic for about 4 minutes.
2. Stir in the thyme and pepper and stir fry for about 3-4 minutes.
3. Meanwhile, in a food processor, add the beans, flour, broth and soy sauce and pulse until pureed.
4. Add the cooked onion mixture and pulse until well combined.
5. In the same pot, add the pureed mixture over medium heat and cook until mixture becomes thick.
6. Se the heat to low and stir in a little water and salt.
7. Enjoy hot..

Croquettes with Cremini Gravy

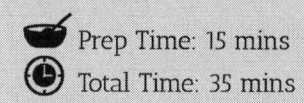

Prep Time: 15 mins
Total Time: 35 mins

Servings per Recipe: 8
Calories   319.7 kcal
Fat   18.5 g
Cholesterol   69.3 mg
Sodium   699.5 mg
Carbohydrates   22.0 g
Protein   16.2 g

Ingredients

1 garlic clove, cracked from skin
1/2 small onion
1 celery rib, chopped
1/4 small red bell pepper, chopped
1 C. chopped cooked turkey, white and dark
1 C. leftover mashed potatoes
1 egg
salt and pepper
2 tsp poultry seasoning
3 sprigs parsley, leaves only
1 C. Italian seasoned breadcrumbs
3 tbsp butter
4 tbsp extra-virgin olive oil
12 cremini mushrooms, sliced
3-4 sprigs rosemary, chopped
2 tbsp all-purpose flour
3 C. chicken stock
1/2 C. grated Romano cheese

Directions

1. In a blender, add the bell pepper, celery, onion and garlic and process until chopped.
2. Add the turkey, potatoes, parsley, egg, poultry seasoning, salt and pepper and process until blended.
3. In a bowl, add the blended turkey mixture and 3/4 C. of the breadcrumbs and mix well.
4. In a skillet, add 1 tbsp. of the oil and 2 tbsp of the butter over medium heat and cook until heated.
5. Add the mushrooms and cook for about 6-7 minutes.
6. Add the rosemary, salt and pepper and stir to combine.
7. Stir in the flour and cook for about 1 minute, stirring continuously.
8. Add the stock, beating continuously and cook until boiling.
9. Set the heat to medium-low and cook for about 5 minutes.
10. With an ice cream scooper, make 8 equal sized croquettes from the turkey mixture.
11. In a shallow bowl, add remaining 1/4 C. of the breadcrumbs and cheese and mix well.

12. Coat the croquettes with the cheese mixture evenly.
13. In another nonstick skillet, add the remaining oil over medium heat and cook until heated.
14. Add the croquettes in batches and cook for about 5-6 minutes.
15. With a slotted spoon, transfer the croquettes onto a paper towel-lined plate to drain.
16. Enjoy the croquettes with a topping of the gravy..

Plain Yogurt Gravy

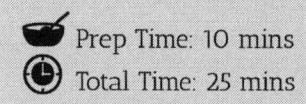

Prep Time: 10 mins
Total Time: 25 mins

Servings per Recipe: 2
Calories	102.3 kcal
Fat	3.4 g
Cholesterol	12.5 mg
Sodium	131.4 mg
Carbohydrates	14.3 g
Protein	5.0 g

Ingredients

- vegetable oil cooking spray
- 4 large mushrooms, chopped
- 1 medium onion, chopped
- 2 oz. plain yogurt
- 1 tbsp Worcestershire sauce
- 1/4 tsp pepper, ground
- 1/2 C. milk
- 1 tsp cornstarch

Directions

1. Grease a nonstick skillet with the cooking spray and heat it.
2. Add the onions and mushrooms and cook for about 5-6 minutes, mixing frequently.
3. Meanwhile, in a bowl, add the yogurt, half of the milk, Worcestershire sauce and pepper and beat until well combined.
4. Add the milk mixture into the skillet, mixing continuously.
5. Cook until boiling and then cook for about 5-6 minutes.
6. In a bowl, dissolve the cornstarch into remaining milk.
7. Add the cornstarch mixture into the skillet, mixing continuously. a
8. Cook until boiling, mixing occasionally.
9. Enjoy hot.

VEGAN
Comfort Food (Biscuits with Gravy)

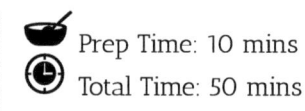

Prep Time: 10 mins
Total Time: 50 mins

Servings per Recipe: 4
Calories	1005.8 kcal
Fat	49.1 g
Cholesterol	12.3 mg
Sodium	2427.6 mg
Carbohydrates	116.0 g
Protein	24.3 g

Ingredients

1 quart all-purpose flour
2 tbsp baking powder
2 tsp salt
3/4 C. margarine
2 C. soy milk
1 tbsp canola oil

1 1/2 tbsp flour
3 tbsp minced garlic
1 tbsp gravy seasoning
2 C. unsweetened soy milk
6 tbsp cooked vegan sausage, diced

Directions

1. For the biscuits: in a bowl, sift together the 1 quart of the flour, baking powder and salt.
2. With a pastry blender, cut the margarine into the flour mixture until well combined.
3. Add the soy milk and with your hands, mix until a slightly wet dough is formed.
4. Place the dough in fridge for about 1 hour.
5. Set your oven to 450 degrees F and lightly, grease a baking sheet.
6. Place the dough onto a floured surface and with your hands, flatten it.
7. Sprinkle the extra flour on top of the dough.
8. with a biscuit cutter, cut the biscuits from the dough.
9. In the bottom of the prepared baking sheet, arrange the biscuits.
10. Cook in the oven for about 25 minutes.
11. For the gravy: heat a skillet and stir fry the sausage for about 5-6 minutes.
12. Transfer the sausage into a bowl and keep aside.
13. Meanwhile, in a pan, add the oil over medium-high heat and cook until heated.
14. Add the garlic and seasoning mix and stir fry for about 1 minute.
15. Add the flour, stirring continuously until smooth.
16. Set the heat to medium-low.

17. Add the soy milk, beating continuously until well combined.
18. Cook until gravy becomes thick, mixing frequently.
19. Add the cooked sausage and stir to combine well.
20. Enjoy the biscuits with a topping of the gravy.

GRAVY
in College

🍲 Prep Time: 5 mins
🕐 Total Time: 25 mins

Servings per Recipe: 4
Calories   265.3 kcal
Fat   23.1 g
Cholesterol   61.0 mg
Sodium   208.3 mg
Carbohydrates   13.0 g
Protein   2.0 g

Ingredients

1/2 C. butter
1/4 C. diced onion
1/4 C. sliced celery
1 1/2 tsp. chopped fresh thyme
1/2 C. all-purpose flour
1 carton (32 oz.) Chicken Broth, divided

Directions

1. For the gravy base: in a pot, add the butter over medium-high heat and cook until melted.
2. Add the celery, onion and thyme and stir fry for about 5-5 minutes.
3. Stir in the flour and cook for about 2-3 minutes, mixing continuously.
4. Slowly, add 2 C. broth, mixing continuously.
5. Cook for about 2-3 minutes, mixing frequently.
6. Remove from the heat and keep aside to cool completely.
7. Place the gravy base and remaining broth until using.
8. After the cooking of turkey in oven, transfer it onto a platter.
9. With a slotted spoon, remove the fat from pan drippings.
10. In a pan, add the turkey pan drippings and gravy base over medium heat and cook until heated through, mixing frequently.
11. Slowly, add the reserved broth, mixing continuously.
12. Cook until desired thickness of the gravy.
13. Enjoy hot..

Dairy-Free Gravy

Prep Time: 10 mins
Total Time: 1 hr 10 mins

Servings per Recipe: 4
Calories   37.8 kcal
Fat   0.7 g
Cholesterol   0.0 mg
Sodium   378.5 mg
Carbohydrates   4.7 g
Protein   2.9 g

Ingredients

2 C. chicken broth
1 leek, sliced
1 garlic clove, minced
1 shallot, sliced
1 tsp salt
1/2 tsp pepper

Directions

1. In a pan, add all the ingredients and cook until boiling.
2. Set the heat to low and cook for about 1 hour.
3. Remove from the heat and with a slotted spoon, remove fat from top surface.
4. With an immersion blender, blend the gravy until desired texture is achieved.
5. Enjoy.
6.

GERMAN
Gingersnap Gravy

Prep Time: 10 mins
Total Time: 30 mins

Servings per Recipe: 12
Calories   338.8 kcal
Fat   24.2 g
Cholesterol   40.1 mg
Sodium   974.3 mg
Carbohydrates 18.7 g
Protein   9.6 g

Ingredients

5 3/4 C. cold water
1 medium onion, chopped
salt and pepper,
33 gingersnap cookies
1 1/2 C. white distilled vinegar
2 lb. sliced all beef wieners

hot-cooked mashed potatoes

Directions

1. In a wok, add the gingersnaps, onion, salt, pepper and water over medium-low heat and cook until the gingersnaps dissolve completely, mixing gently.
2. Add the sliced wieners and vinegar and cook until just boiling, mixing frequently.
3. Cook for about 10 minutes, mixing frequently.
4. Set the heat to low and simmer for about 12-15 minutes.
5. Enjoy hot..Z

Pan Fried Gravy

Prep Time: 5 mins
Total Time: 15 mins

Servings per Recipe: 4
Calories	159.5 kcal
Fat	11.3 g
Cholesterol	17.0 mg
Sodium	59.9 mg
Carbohydrates	10.1 g
Protein	4.6 g

Ingredients

2 tbsp unsalted butter
3 - 4 tbsp flour
2 C. milk
salt & pepper

Directions

1. In a pan, add the butter over medium heat and cook until melted.
2. Slowly, add the flour, beating continuously until smooth.
3. Cook until a smooth paste is formed, stirring continuously.
4. Set the heat to medium-low.
5. Slowly, add the milk, beating continuously until smooth.
6. Set the heat to medium and cook until desired thickness of the sauce, mixing continuously.
7. Stir in the salt and pepper and enjoy.

MEXICAN
Chocolate Gravy

🥣 Prep Time: 5 mins
🕐 Total Time: 20 mins

Servings per Recipe: 4
Calories   254.5 kcal
Fat   12.2 g
Cholesterol   31.2 mg
Sodium   247.1 mg
Carbohydrates   33.7 g
Protein   5.9 g

Ingredients

1/3 C. unsweetened cocoa powder
3 tbsp all-purpose flour
2/3 C. powdered sugar
2 C. whole milk
2 1/2 tbsp butter
1 tsp vanilla

1/4 tsp salt
cayenne pepper

Directions

1. In a wok, melt the butter over medium-low heat.
2. Slowly, add the flour, beating continuously until smooth.
3. Add the sugar and chocolate and beat until well combined.
4. Cook for about 2 minutes, stirring continuously.
5. Slowly, add the milk, beating continuously until smooth.
6. Stir in the cayenne, salt and vanilla and
7. cook for about 2-4 minutes.
8. Enjoy hot..

Curried Seafood Gravy

Prep Time: 5 mins
Total Time: 25 mins

Servings per Recipe: 4
Calories	132.9 kcal
Fat	1.6 g
Cholesterol	97.5 mg
Sodium	370.9 mg
Carbohydrates	5.1 g
Protein	23.4 g

Ingredients

- 1/2 kg cleaned crab, outer shell removed
- 1 sprig curry leaf
- 1 tsp mustard seeds
- 1 tsp garam masala
- 1 tsp red chili pepper
- 2 tsp coriander powder
- 1 tsp ginger-garlic paste
- 1 large onion, chopped
- 1 tomatoes, chopped
- cooking oil
- 1/2 C. water

Directions

1. In a skillet, add the oil and cook until heated.
2. Add the mustard seeds and stir fry for about 30 seconds.
3. Add the onions, ginger-garlic paste and curry leaves and stir fry for about 5 minutes.
4. Add the tomatoes, garam masala, coriander and chili pepper and stir to combine.
5. Stir in the water and cook for about 4-5 minutes.
6. Stir in the crabs, salt and a little water and cook, covered for about 5 minutes.
7. Uncover and stir fry for about 10 minutes.
8. Enjoy hot.

APRIL
Egg Gravy

🥣 Prep Time: 30 mins
🕐 Total Time: 1 hr

Servings per Recipe: 1
Calories	376.8 kcal
Fat	29.8 g
Cholesterol	247.5 mg
Sodium	1592.9 mg
Carbohydrates	13.4 g
Protein	13.0 g

Ingredients

1/2 C. butter, melted
1/2 C. all-purpose flour
1 tsp salt
4 C. hot chicken broth
1 chicken giblets, cooked and chopped
4 hard-boiled eggs, chopped

Directions

1. In a pot, add the flour, butter and salt over low heat and mix until smooth.
2. Slowly, add the chicken broth, stirring continuously.
3. Add the eggs and chicken giblets and simmer until desired thickness, mixing continuously.
4. Enjoy hot..

Garlicky Spuds with Gravy

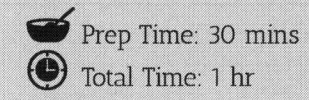

Prep Time: 30 mins
Total Time: 1 hr

Servings per Recipe: 8
Calories	447.9 kcal
Fat	29.0 g
Cholesterol	0.0 mg
Sodium	994.0 mg
Carbohydrates	40.6 g
Protein	9.3 g

Ingredients

Potatoes
6 large baking potatoes, peeled and diced
2 tsp vegetable oil
10 cloves garlic, minced
1 1/2 C. soy milk
6 tbsp soy margarine
Gravy
1/2 C. nutritional yeast
6 tbsp margarine
1 medium onion
6 tbsp flour
1 1/4 C. ground cashews
4 C. vegetarian chicken broth
5 tbsp tamari
3 cloves crushed garlic
pepper

Directions

1. In a pan of the boiling water, cook the potatoes until soft.
2. In a pan, add the oil over medium heat and cook until heated.
3. Add the garlic and stir fry for about 40 seconds.
4. Add the soy milk and stir to combine.
5. Set the heat to low and cook until warmed through.
6. Drain the potatoes well and transfer into a bowl.
7. With a potato masher, mash the potatoes well.
8. Add the margarine and stir to combine.
9. Add the nutritional yeast and soy milk mixture and stir until well combined.
10. For the gravy: in a pan, melt the margarine and stir fry the onions for about 6-8 minutes.
11. Stir in the cashews and flour and cook for about 2-3 minutes, mixing continuously.
12. Slowly, add the broth, beating continuously until smooth.
13. Add the garlic, soy sauce and pepper and cook until boiling.
14. Set the heat to low and cook until desired thickness of the gravy.
15. Remove from the heat and with a hand blender, blend until smooth.
16. Place the gravy over the mashed potatoes and enjoy.

5-INGREDIENT Gravy

Prep Time: 5 mins
Total Time: 15 mins

Servings per Recipe: 4
Calories	48.8 kcal
Fat	1.9 g
Cholesterol	0.7 mg
Sodium	478.0 mg
Carbohydrates	4.2 g
Protein	3.3 g

Ingredients

1 can Swanson chicken broth
1 herb-ox beef flavor cube
1 tsp olive oil
2 tbsp cornstarch
4 tbsp water

Directions

1. Shake the can of stock well.
2. In a pan, add the oil, beef cube and stock and cook until boiling.
3. In a bowl, dissolve the corn starch into 4 tbsp of the water.
4. Add the corn starch mixture and beat until well combined.
5. Cook until desired thickness of the gravy.
6. Enjoy hot..

Birmingham Gravy

Prep Time: 5 mins
Total Time: 15 mins

Servings per Recipe: 6
Calories	86.8 kcal
Fat	7.8 g
Cholesterol	20.3 mg
Sodium	172.4 mg
Carbohydrates	3.7 g
Protein	1.0 g

Ingredients

2 oz. butter
1 small onion, chopped
4 oz. sliced mushrooms
1 bouillon cube
300 ml hot water
2 tbsp corn flour, blended with a little cold water

salt and black pepper

Directions

1. In a pan, add the butter and cook until melted.
2. Add the mushrooms and onion and cook for about 7-8 minutes.
3. In a bowl, add the stock cube and hot water and mix well.
4. Add the stock cube mixture into the pan and stir to combine.
5. Stir in the corn flour mixture and cook until desired thickness, mixing continuously.
6. Enjoy hot.

45-MINUTE Chicken with Gravy

Prep Time: 10 mins
Total Time: 45 mins

Servings per Recipe: 4
Calories   850.1 kcal
Fat   68.8 g
Cholesterol   247.7 mg
Sodium   317.7 mg
Carbohydrates   7.7 g
Protein   48.5 g

Ingredients

2 tbsp unsalted butter
1 whole chicken, cut
salt and pepper
1/2 tsp rosemary
1 C. hot chicken stock
2 1/3 C. sour cream

Directions

1. Set your oven to 325 degrees F before doing anything else.
2. In an oven-proof, add the butter and cook until melted.
3. Add the chicken and cook until browned completely.
4. Add the rosemary, salt, pepper and stock over the chicken.
5. Cook in the oven for about 35 minutes.
6. Remove from the oven and transfer the pan juices into a pan over high heat and cook until it reduces to 1/2 C.
7. Add the sour cream and stir to combine well.
8. Transfer the chicken onto a platter and enjoy with a topping of the gravy..

Baked Chicken Cutlets with Gravy

Prep Time: 15 mins
Total Time: 1 hr

Servings per Recipe: 4
Calories	321.2 kcal
Fat	17.1 g
Cholesterol	99.8 mg
Sodium	450.6 mg
Carbohydrates	12.8 g
Protein	27.3 g

Ingredients

- 1/2 C. all-purpose flour
- 2 egg whites, lightly beaten
- 1 1/3 C. cornflake cereal, crushed
- 2 bone-in chicken breast halves, skinned
- 2 chicken drumsticks, skinned
- 2 chicken thighs, skinned
- 1/2 tsp salt
- 1/8 tsp cayenne pepper
- 1/4 C. fat-free buttermilk
- 1 tbsp butter
- 1 C. reduced-sodium chicken broth
- 1/4 tsp dried sage
- 1/8 tsp black pepper

Directions

1. Set your oven to 375 degrees F before doing anything else and arrange a greased wire rack in a foil lined baking dish.
2. In 3 different shallow dishes, place 1/2 cup flour in, beaten egg whites and cornflake crumbs respectively.
3. In a bowl, add chicken, buttermilk, salt and cayenne pepper and mix well.
4. Coat the chicken pieces with the flour, then dip in egg whites and finally, coat with the cornflake crumbs evenly.
5. Arrange the chicken pieces oven the rack in baking dish and spray with the cooking spray.
6. Cook in the oven for about 45 minutes.
7. Meanwhile, for the gravy: in a pan, add the butter over medium-high heat and cook until melted.
8. Stir in the remaining 2 tbsp of the flour and cook for about 1 minute, beating continuously.
9. Slowly, add the chicken broth, beating continuously.
10. Cook for about 2 minutes, beating continuously.
11. Stir in the sage and black pepper and remove from the heat.
12. Enjoy the chicken pieces alongside the gravy.

AMELIA'S
Turkey with Country Gravy

🥣 Prep Time: 45 mins
🕐 Total Time: 2 hrs 45 mins

Servings per Recipe: 1
Calories	208.9 kcal
Fat	2.8 g
Cholesterol	0.0 mg
Sodium	266.8 mg
Carbohydrates	36.9 g
Protein	9.7 g

Ingredients

Brine
8 C. apple cider
2/3 C. kosher salt
2/3 C. sugar
1 tbsp black peppercorns, crushed
1 tbsp whole allspice, crushed
8 ginger, slices, peeled
6 whole cloves
2 bay leaves
1 turkey
2 oranges
6 C. ice
Spiced
4 garlic cloves
4 sage leaves
4 thyme, springs
4 parsley sprigs
1 onion, quartered
1 (14 oz.) cans chicken broth
2 tbsp unsalted butter, melted and divided
1 tsp black pepper, divided
1/2 tsp salt, divided
Gravy
2 tsp vegetable oil
turkey neck, and giblets
4 C. water
6 black peppercorns
4 parsley sprigs
2 thyme sprigs
1 yellow onion, unpeeled and quartered
1 carrot, chopped
1 celery, chopped
1 bay leaf
reserved turkey drippings
3 tbsp all-purpose flour
1/2 tsp salt
1/4 tsp salt
1/4 tsp black pepper

Directions

1. For the brine: in a pot, add the apple cider, ginger, sugar, salt, black peppercorns, whole allspice, whole cloves and bay leaves and cook until boiling.
2. Cook for about 5 minutes, stirring frequently.
3. Remove from the heat and keep aside to cool completely.
4. Remove the neck and giblets from turkey and reserve for the gravy.

5. Rinse the turkey under cold running water and with paper towels pat dry it.
6. Trim the excess fat from turkey.
7. Stuff the cavity of the turkey with the orange quarters.
8. Arrange a larger re-sealable bag inside a another larger bag to for double thickness.
9. Now, arrange the bags in a pan.
10. In the inner bag, place the turkey, brine mixture and ice.
11. Seal the bags and place in the fridge for about 13-24 hours, flipping occasionally.
12. Set your oven to 500 degrees F.
13. Remove the turkey from bags and discard the orange quarters.
14. Rinse the turkey under cold running water and with paper towels pat dry it.
15. Tuck the wings under turkey and then, with kitchen strings, tie the legs together.
16. In a roasting pan, place the onion, garlic, parsley, thyme, sage and broth.
17. Now, arrange a rack in the roasting pan.
18. Place the turkey over rack, breast side down.
19. Coat the turkey back with 1 tbsp of the butter and sprinkle with 1/4 tsp of the salt and 1/2 tsp of the pepper.
20. Cook in the oven for about 30 minutes.
21. Now, set the oven to 350 degrees F.
22. Remove the turkey from oven and change the side of turkey.
23. Coat the turkey breast with 1 tbsp of the butter and sprinkle with 1/4 tsp of the salt and 1/2 tsp of the pepper.
24. Cook in the oven for about 1 1/4 hours.
25. Remove the turkey from oven and place onto a platter for about 20 minutes before carving.
26. Reserve the pan mixture for the gravy.
27. For the gravy: in a pan, add the oil over medium-high heat and cook until heated.
28. Add the turkey neck and giblets and sear for about 4-5 minutes.
29. Add the peppercorns, herb sprigs, onion, carrot, celery, bay leaf and water and cook until boiling.
30. Set the heat to low and cook for about 1 hour.
31. Through a strainer, strain the cooking liquid into a bowl, reserving turkey neck.
32. Discard the remaining solids.
33. Refrigerate the cooking liquid until chilled completely.
34. With a slotted spoon, remove the fat from top surface.
35. Remove the meat from neck and then, chop .
36. Discard the bone.

37. Add neck meat to cooking liquid.
38. Through a strainer, strain the reserved turkey drippings in a bowl, discarding the solids.
39. Freeze the strained drippings for about 20 minutes.
40. With a slotted spoon, remove the fat from top surface.
41. In a pan, add the flour and 1/4 cup of the cooking liquid, mixing continuously until smooth.
42. Add the turkey drippings, remaining cooking liquid, salt and pepper and cook until boiling, mixing frequently.
43. Set the heat to low and cook for about 4-5 minutes.
44. Enjoy hot..

Japanese Mushroom Gravy

🍳 Prep Time: 10 mins
🕐 Total Time: 45 mins

Servings per Recipe: 1
Calories   73.7 kcal
Fat   0.4 g
Cholesterol   0.0 mg
Sodium   504.3 mg
Carbohydrates   15.6 g
Protein   3.4 g

Ingredients

- 1/4-1/3 C. olive oil
- 1/2 C. whole wheat flour
- 1/4 lb. shiitake mushroom, sliced
- 2 tbsp thyme
- 1 quart vegetable stock
- 2 tbsp soy sauce
- 1 tsp apple cider vinegar
- sea salt
- ground black pepper

Directions

1. In a pot, add the oil and cook until heated.
2. Add the flour, mixing continuously until smooth.
3. Stir in the mushrooms and cook for about 6 minutes.
4. Stir in the soy sauce and stock and cook until boiling.
5. Cook for about 25-30 minutes, stirring frequently.
6. Stir in the apple cider vinegar, salt and black pepper and remove from the heat.
7. Enjoy hot.

NUTTY
Garlic Gravy

Prep Time: 15 mins
Total Time: 1 hr

Servings per Recipe: 12
Calories	152.4 kcal
Fat	11.7 g
Cholesterol	0.0 mg
Sodium	314.2 mg
Carbohydrates	9.7 g
Protein	4.0 g

Ingredients

1 tbsp oil
1 onion, chopped
2 C. raw cashews
3 garlic cloves, crushed
2 tbsp flour
2 tbsp soy sauce

salt and pepper

Directions

1. In a skillet, heat the oil and stir fry the onion for about 5-7 minutes.
2. Stir in the cashews and cook until toasted completely.
3. Add the garlic and cook for about 1 minute.
4. Stir in the flour and cook for about 1 minute.
5. Add the water in 2 batches, stirring continuously until smooth.
6. Add 1-2 C. of the water, soy sauce, salt and pepper and simmer for about 29-30 minutes.
7. Remove from the heat and keep aside for about 4-5 minutes to cool.
8. In a food processor, add the cashew mixture and pulse until smooth.
9. Enjoy hot..

Mushroom Gravy

Prep Time: 30 mins
Total Time: 30 mins

Servings per Recipe: 8
Calories	33.9 kcal
Fat	1.7 g
Cholesterol	0.0 mg
Sodium	378.7 mg
Carbohydrates	3.7 g
Protein	1.2 g

Ingredients

- 1 tbsp extra-virgin olive oil
- 1 medium onion, chopped
- 2 garlic cloves, minced
- 1 1/2 C. chopped cleaned portabella mushrooms
- 2 1/4 C. vegetable broth
- 3 tbsp tamari
- 1/4 tsp dried thyme leaves
- 1/8 tsp crumbled dried sage
- 1 tbsp cornstarch
- 2 tbsp water
- fresh ground pepper

Directions

1. In a pot, add the oil over medium heat and cook until heated through.
2. Add the garlic and onion and cook for about 4-6 minutes, mixing occasionally.
3. Stir in the mushrooms and cook for about 8-9 minutes, mixing occasionally.
4. Stir in the sage, thyme, tamari and broth and cook for about 9-10 minutes.
5. In a bowl, dissolve the cornstarch in water.
6. Add the cornstarch mixture into the pot, stirring continuously.
7. Cook for about 9-10 minutes, mixing occasionally.
8. Stir in the pepper and remove from the heat.
9. With a slotted spoon, remove the onion and mushrooms.
10. Enjoy hot.

CORNED Beef with Irish Gravy

🥣 Prep Time: 40 mins
🕐 Total Time: 5 hrs

Servings per Recipe: 8
Calories 647.5 kcal
Fat 39.8 g
Cholesterol 168.7 mg
Sodium 3422.3 mg
Carbohydrates 31.0 g
Protein 39.1 g

Ingredients

- 3 - 4 lb. corned beef brisket
- 1 tbsp canola oil
- 3 diced carrots
- 3 carrots, quartered lengthwise
- 1 medium onion, chopped
- 1 medium onion, quartered
- 2 celery ribs, diced
- 1/4 C. packed dark brown sugar
- 1 1/2 tsp dried thyme
- 2 C. ale
- 1 - 2 tbsp Dijon mustard
- 1 small head of cabbage, cut into wedges

Gravy
- 1/2 C. milk
- 1 tsp Dijon mustard
- 3 - 4 tbsp prepared horseradish, squeezed dry
- 1 C. corned beef, cooking liquid
- 3/4 tsp dried thyme
- 1/2 tsp pepper
- 4 tsp cornstarch
- 2 tbsp minced parsley

Directions

1. Season the corned beef with the black pepper.
2. Place a Dutch oven over high heat until heated through.
3. Add the corned beef and cook for about 6 minutes.
4. Transfer the beef into a bowl and keep aside.
5. Set the heat to medium.
6. Add the celery, diced carrots, chopped onion, thyme and brown sugar and stir fry for about 7 minutes.
7. Set the heat to low.
8. Stir in the mustard and ale and cook for about 2 minutes, stirring continuously.
9. Stir in the cooked beef and simmer, covered for about 3 1/2 hours.
10. Add the quartered onions, sliced carrots, cabbage and simmer, covered for about 39 - 41

minutes.
11. With a slotted spoon, transfer the beef onto a cutting board for about 15 minutes.
12. With a slotted spoon, transfer the large vegetable and cabbage pieces onto a serving platter and with a piece of foil, cover then to keep warm.
13. For the gravy: through a strainer, strain the pan juices in a bowl.
14. With a slotted spoon, remove the fat from the top.
15. In a pan, add horseradish, milk, 1 C. of the strained juices, mustard, thyme and pepper over medium heat.
16. In a bowl, add 2 tbsp of the reserved horseradish liquid and cornstarch and stir to combine well.
17. Stir the cornstarch mixture into the pan, and cook for about 3 minutes, mixing continuously.
18. Remove from the heat and stir in the parsley.
19. Cut the corned beef into desired sized slices.
20. Enjoy the beef and vegetables alongside the gravy..

RED
Gravy

🥣 Prep Time: 30 mins
🕒 Total Time: 6 hrs 35 mins

Servings per Recipe: 20
Calories	5.6 kcal
Fat	0.4 g
Cholesterol	0.0 mg
Sodium	0.2 mg
Carbohydrates	0.3 g
Protein	0.0 g

Ingredients

5 cans Cento Italian tomatoes
6 cloves garlic
2 lb. prosciutto ham, cubed
5 2 tsp good virgin olive oil
1 tsp basil
1 tsp crushed red pepper flakes

Directions

1. In a food processor, add the tomatoes and pulse until smooth.
2. In a pan, heat the oil and stir fry the
3. garlic for about 30-40 seconds.
4. Add the ham, pureed tomatoes, basil and red pepper flakes and stir to combine.
5. Reduce the heat to low and cook for about 6 hours.
6. Enjoy hot..

Apple Roasted Turkey with Vinegar Gravy

 Prep Time: 30 mins
 Total Time: 3 hrs 30 mins

Servings per Recipe: 12
Calories   896.6 kcal
Fat   48.1 g
Cholesterol   342.6 mg
Sodium   709.0 mg
Carbohydrates   15.9 g
Protein   94.3 g

Ingredients

1/2 C. apple jelly
1/2 C. butter
2 tbsp coarse-grained Dijon mustard
1 tbsp ground black pepper
1/2 tsp salt
12 lb. turkey, giblets and neck removed and pat dried
1 medium granny smith apple, quartered
1 medium onion, quartered
parsley sprig
1 tsp pepper
1/4 tsp salt
Vinegar Gravy
1/2 C. reserved pan dripping
1/4 C. all-purpose flour
1 (14 1/2 oz.) cans chicken broth
1 C. apple cider
1/2 C. whipping cream
1/2 tsp pepper
1/4 tsp salt

Directions

1. Set your oven to 325 degrees F before doing anything else and arrange a wire rack in a roasting pan.
2. For the glaze: in a pan, add the apple jelly, butter, Dijon mustard, salt and black pepper over medium heat and cook until jelly melts completely, stirring continuously.
3. Stuff the turkey cavity with the onion, apple and parsley sprigs.
4. Place turkey over the rack in the roasting pan, breast side up.
5. Coat the turkey with half of the glaze evenly and season with 1/4 tsp of the salt and 1 tsp of the pepper.
6. Cook in the oven for about 3 hours.
7. After 30 minutes of the cooking, cover the turkey with the foil.
8. After 1 1/2 hours, coat the turkey with the remaining glaze.
9. Remove turkey from the oven and place onto a platter for about 10 minutes before carving.
10. For the gravy: Transfer the pan drippings into a pot over medium heat.

11. Add the flour, beating continuously.
12. Cook for about 1 minute, beating continuously.
13. Stir in the whipping cream, chicken broth and apple cider and cook until desired thickness of gravy.
14. Stir in the salt and pepper and remove from the heat.
15. Enjoy the turkey alongside the gravy.

ENJOY THE RECIPES?

KEEP ON COOKING WITH 6 MORE FREE COOKBOOKS!

Visit our website and simply enter your email address to join the club and receive your 6 cookbooks.

http://booksumo.com/magnet

https://www.instagram.com/booksumopress/

https://www.facebook.com/booksumo/

Printed in Great Britain
by Amazon